# Seas[illegible]

# Safaris



## Exploring rocky and sandy seashores with Judith Oakley

GRAFFEG

# Contents


Foreword by Iolo Williams 4
Foreword by Keith Hiscock 6
Introduction by Judith Oakley 8

**1. Getting started 12**

About this book 12
Equipment checklist 13
Health and Safety matters 14
The Seashore Code 15
Where to look 16
Record your findings 17

**2. Living between the tides 18**

Forces shaping the shore 20
Rocky and sandy shores 22
Survival on the shore 24
Eat or be eaten (food chains and webs) 25

**3. Zonation 26**

Rocky shore zonation 28
Splash zone 30
Upper shore 32
Middle shore 34
Lower shore 36
Laminarian zone 38
Sandy shore zonation 40

**4. Habitats 42**

Crevices 44
Surge gullies 46
Overhangs 48
Rockpools 50
On and under seaweed 52
On boulders 54
Under boulders 56
Strandline 58
In and on sand 60
In pools and on the strandline 62
Signs of life and quiz 64

**5. Beachcombing 68**

Stranded creatures 70
Strandline treasures – shell guide 72
Assorted strandline treasures 74

**6. Animal life 76**

**Porifera or sponges** 78
**Cnidaria** (Hydroids or sea firs, corals and sea anemones) 82
**Worms** 94
**Crustaceans** (Barnacles, crabs, lobsters, prawns, shrimps, and sandy shore crabs) 104
**Molluscs** (Chitons, sea snails, sea slugs and bivalves) 120
**Bryozoans or sea mats** 150
**Echinoderms** (Sea cucumbers, crinoids, starfish, brittlestars, sea urchins and sandy shore echinoderms) 152
**Tunicates and vertebrates** (Sea squirts and fish) 166
**Who laid these eggs?** 180

**7. Seaweeds 184**

Seaweed zonation 186
Green algae 188
Brown algae 190
Red algae 196

**8. Conservation 200**

Threats to our shores 202
Beach litter and quiz 204
Non-native species 206
How you can help 210
Where to report your findings 212

Further information 214
Glossary 216
Acknowledgements 220
Index 221
Animal life quick reference key 225

# Foreword Iolo Williams

**There is nothing quite as exciting as exploring the seashore. Whether you're 3 or 103, you can't fail to feel that rush of anticipation when you stare into a rockpool or rummage underneath some seaweed, looking for a crab, a shrimp or something even more exotic.**

It's the same feeling as you get when you wake up on Christmas morning – you never know what you're going to find.

Iolo at Oxwich Bay with a Moon jellyfish

Iolo and Judith

The creatures that live along our shores are well adapted to a harsh environment. They have to be able to withstand crashing waves, sea and fresh water, hot and cold temperatures and a myriad of predators, as well as inquisitive *Homo sapiens*. Because of this, they come in a weird and wonderful array of shapes and colours, from the sublime to the ridiculous.

We're so lucky in Wales to have some of the best seashores in the world and now, we have a top class guidebook to help us to enjoy them.

From my own experiences, I know how frustrating it can be to explore a rockpool without really knowing what you're looking at.

Over the years, thanks to experts like Judith, I have gradually come to recognise an increasing number of these incredible creatures, and the more I learn, the more I want to know.

Is there much life on a sandy shore?

What does a pipefish look like?

Have I got porcelain crabs on my local beach?

This guidebook will help you to answer all of these questions and a whole lot more. One of conservation's biggest successes over the past 50 years has been education. Our children are far more aware of the importance of our environment than we ever were. This guidebook will help to ensure that future generations continue to enjoy and respect our seashore life for decades to come.

**Iolo Williams**
Broadcaster and Naturalist

Snake pipefish

Broad-clawed porcelain crab

# Foreword Keith Hiscock

**Everyone who enjoys exploring the sea shore will constantly find some new treasure or see some new, often amazing, facet of wildlife. Being able to put names to what you see and, better still, to use your observations to add to our knowledge about the natural world is what this book is about.**

Keith Hiscock, marine biologist, diver and underwater photographer

Angular crab

Judith Oakley has an infectious enthusiasm for marine species and ecology that comes to life here in words and pictures, informing and exciting the reader about the enormous range of wildlife on our shores. After exploring the shore a few times, you'll become familiar with the widespread species and should start to see more unusual, sometimes rare, species. As you explore, think about how marine life changes with the seasons, how pollution, climate change and non-native species might affect our native wildlife – and remember to record what you see. So, do follow Judith on a trail of discovery that will enrich your life and help you to appreciate what marvels we have on our shores.

Beadlet anemone

**Dr Keith Hiscock**
Associate Fellow of the Marine Biological Association and former Programme Director of the Marine Life Information Network (*MarLIN*).

Spiny starfish

Shore clingfish

# Introduction Judith Oakley

**'Seashore Safaris' is intended as a photographic guide, documenting the intriguing tiny animals you can find if you look carefully in the right places on a rocky or sandy shore.**

It should inspire you to venture from the comfort of your deckchair, or from behind your windbreak or computer screen, to explore the richness of life between the tides – the intertidal zone.

Investigating rockpools on Skomer Island

Early days of rockpooling with my brother, Isles of Scilly 1972

*"Why not, then, try to discover a few of the Wonders of the Shore? For wonders there are around you at every step ... and yet to be seen at no greater expense than a very little time and trouble."*
***Glaucus; or The Wonders of the Shore*, Charles Kingsley, 1855**

As an island people we know that much of our history is bound up with the sea. And most of us are not too far from a seashore. In Georgian times, the late seventeenth and early eighteenth centuries, wealthy people started having seaside holidays for their health, and saltwater cures for their ailments. In the Victorian years natural history became a relatively popular hobby and people started dabbling in rockpools. Philip Henry Gosse was one of the pioneering naturalists of this period, author of various works on marine biology, and inventor of the marine aquarium. He brought the study of nature to public attention, and amongst many Victorians, inspired an enthusiasm for seashore safaris, rockpool rambles and coastal expeditions. Gosse, typically dressed in a large hat and long coat, armed with his collecting baskets, led many guided tours of the shore for the middle classes. He was aided by his friend Charles Kingsley, who himself spent much time in Devon investigating seashore flora, fauna and geology. This led to the publication of a series of articles in the North British Review, later published as Glaucus; or The Wonders of the Shore, which he also illustrated. Kingsley and Gosse would spend many months away on their seaside excursions, so only an elite group could join them. They made an immense contribution to the advancement of our understanding of seashore life. The growth in public interest in aspects of marine zoology led to the formation of the Conchological Society in 1876 and the Marine Biological Association of Great Britain eight years later. The latter organization is one with which I maintain a fruitful working relationship.

Fortunately, the seashore habitat is no longer the domain of only those with a privileged status. It is accessible for us all to enjoy, and to explore its hidden secrets. Like the Victorians, I began my seashore interest as an amateur naturalist, and rocky shores in particular have fascinated me for many years. I spent my childhood living close to the sea in south Wales, and enjoyed exploring the seashore with my parents and my brother at an early age.
I have sustained this interest and passion for over 35 years, and I am still enticed by extreme spring tides and the treasures they uncover. Unlike the Victorians, however, who were avid collectors of hundreds of specimens from the shore, I investigate the wealth of hidden wildlife with my camera, eyes and notebook. Rocky shores

provide unique mini-habitats in the form of rockpools, overhangs, crevices, surge gullies, boulders and amongst seaweeds, where an extraordinary array of creatures can be found. Sandy shores are also teeming with wildlife hidden in the sediment. There is immense excitement in going out at low tides, and not knowing what I may find to photograph or record on a particular expedition. In the same way as Gosse led many tours of the shore, I am also involved in marine education and awareness raising, and lead walks and talks regularly with public and school groups. However, my safaris are open to all ages and abilities.

The book is not intended solely as an identification guide, but as a general overview of the prolific life to be found on our shores. My main endeavour is to bring the shore to you by means of stunning images, to entice you to rekindle those childhood rockpooling and beachcombing memories, and to help you to rediscover a sense of amazement and awe for the wealth of wildlife on the beaches close to you. The seashore is the one area of the sea that all of us can explore at no cost, and I hope that I can share my enthusiasm and fascination for our shores with you through this book.

You can help marine conservation and marine scientists by becoming a volunteer recorder, and noting what you see on each Seashore Safari. This information is vital in monitoring changes in types of species found and their abundance on our shores.

In the UK, no-one lives more than 120 km from the sea, and the total length of the UK coastline is some 18,838 km. With so much coastline to be discovered, what are you waiting for?

---

**Notes:**

As the work of this book represents a personal account, the species described are limited to those that I have encountered on my own seashore safaris. There are of course many more species, but those included could reasonably be considered a representative selection.

My featured photographs were taken during five years of seashore safaris. I must emphasise that I have striven to show the creatures in their true natural habitat on the shore, going about their daily lives. Most of the images were taken with a Canon digital compact or SLR camera through the water surface and not underwater. In the past year I have been fortunate enough to acquire a compact Canon Ixus 90 IS model and underwater housing, due to very generous sponsorship from Cameras Underwater (www.camerasunderwater.co.uk) enabling me to add a new dimension to my photographs, especially in rockpools.

The challenge, of course, with any shore photography is dealing with shadows, reflections, suspended matter in the water, refraction and manoeuvring the camera and oneself into small and awkward spaces, together with keeping sand and water out of the camera equipment. I am an enthusiastic amateur photographer, but I hope that I have succeeded in capturing shore life in a way that will inspire you to find out more.

This edition is fully revised, with additional images and contains details of a further 16 species.

Interview with Radio Scilly about seashore life

Seashore safari, Newton Point, Porthcawl

Marine education project, Aberafan Beach, Port Talbot

# 1. Getting started

**Just like an African safari to look at wild game animals, a seashore safari involves patience, stealth and a sense of adventure to search for the hidden wildlife on our shores.**

A safari should conjure up images of exploration, excitement, anticipation and a trek to find the wildlife. That is certainly what you will experience on a rocky or sandy shore in Britain or Ireland as you learn to search in the right places for creatures and plants that you may not have seen before. The quick key to animal life (inside back cover) will aid in identification.

To keep safe, and to make sure that you are properly prepared for your safari, and learn the most from it, some key hints and tips are highlighted that should make it a memorable experience.

## About this book

This pocket guide covers many of the more 'common' intertidal species you may encounter on a rocky or sandy shore. It is designed to be taken with you on your low tide seashore safaris for quick reference. However, there will be variations in the species found on each shore, and in the north of the country compared with the south. 'Seashore Safaris' can be used to investigate the different zones of the shore, the many micro-habitats and the associated flora and fauna of both rocky and sandy shores. The book gives basic background information on factors affecting shore life and how the inhabitants are distributed along the shore in zones. Animal and seaweed species are shown in vivid images, together with details regarding size, colour, most likely location and any distinguishing features.

The book outlines the threats to our marine life, with many suggestions about the action you can take to help conserve our shores.'Seashore Safaris' also includes small projects and quizzes that you can undertake to test your knowledge and develop your skills. Some of the more scientific terms are highlighted in bold and definitions of these are included in the glossary. Although the guide may not answer all your questions about life on rocky and sandy shores, it is intended to provide a firm foundation, encouraging you to find out more and develop your interest. Details are included of some of the most informative literature currently available, together with useful websites and organisations which rely on volunteer recorders.

# Equipment checklist

Depending on the weather and the location of your safari, you may find some of the following equipment useful.

**1** Warm hat
**2** Waterproof jacket
**3** Backpack
**4** Foldable shovel
**5** Waterproof trousers
**6** Sieve
**7** Mini-aquarium
**8** White tray
**9** First aid kit
**10** Notebook and pencil
**11** Sealable plastic bags
**12** Small fork or trowel
**13** Magnifying glass
**14** Digital camera
**15** White bucket
**16** Collecting pots
**17** Mobile phone
**18** Small towel
**19** Knee pads
**20** Suntan lotion
**21** Waterproof shoes
**22** Small torch

1. Getting started

# Health and Safety matters

**It is essential that you keep safe on your seashore safari, so the following tips should help:**

- **Always check the local tide times**, and know how long you have before the tide starts to turn. It is always best to follow a falling tide, rather than be chased by an incoming one!
- **Check the weather forecast**
- **Wear suitable clothing and footwear**
- **Beware of slippery seaweed** and sharp barnacles on the rocks!
- **Carry a mobile phone**, or know exactly where the nearest telephone is situated
- **Carry a First Aid kit**
- **Always tell someone where you are going,** and when you estimate you will be back
- **Know where the nearest casualty department is**
- **Carry some form of personal identification**
- If you are a student undertaking fieldwork, carry out a **Risk Assessment of your shore**
- **Be careful when handling creatures** such as crabs, which can give you a painful nip
- **Avoid touching stinging animals**, such as sea anemones and jellyfish, particularly if you are allergic to bee or wasp stings
- **Do not touch any suspicious objects** washed up on the beach, particularly metal canisters and needles. These should be reported to the coastguard or beach lifeguard
- **Stay away from unstable cliffs**
- **Beware of venturing out on soft and sticky mud flats**
- **Always wash your hands** before you eat your packed lunch!

Wear suitable clothing

Avoid touching stinging animals

# The Seashore Code

**Now that you are ready for your safari, please ensure that you follow the Seashore Code on every expedition. It is critical that you treat the creatures, seaweeds and habitats you encounter with respect.**

1 **Always place overturned boulders** and rocks back where you found them and the right way up

2 **Handle creatures with care and respect**, and always wet your hands first

3 **Only place one creature at a time** in a bucket or tray to observe it more closely, and always fill the bucket with sea water

4 **Do not leave any animal in a bucket** or tray for too long, as the water will become too warm, and oxygen levels will drop

5 **Always place creatures back** where you found them, as this is their home and they may also be guarding eggs

6 **Be careful not to trample any creatures** – tread lightly

7 **Never use a net**, as this can damage delicate creatures

8 **Do not kick or prise creatures** off the rocks, as this may kill them

9 **Do not prod soft bodied creatures**, such as sea anemones

10 **If you take shells home**, make sure that they are empty, as they may still contain live sea snails or hermit crabs

11 **Take all your litter home**

Always wet your hands first

Place creatures back where you found them

## 1. Getting started

# Where to look

There are many areas to search on a rocky shore. You could try looking in the places shown in pictures 1 to 6 below. On sandy shores, there are fewer places for animals to hide. You may find pools in which to look, otherwise look closely on the surface of the sand **(7)** for signs of life. You could also try digging carefully, and sieving the sand, to see what may be hiding there **(8)**. Detailed descriptions of rocky and sandy shore habitats are given in Chapter 4 (page 42).

1. In sediment under boulders

2. On and under boulders

3. On and under seaweed

4. In rockpools

5. In surge gullies

6. Under overhangs

# Record your findings

Becoming a volunteer recorder is great fun and very worthwhile. Each time you visit the shore, make notes on what you find, and take photographs if possible.

In your field notebook you should include the date, the time, weather, height of the tide and the location. It is useful also to include a grid reference. Record all the species you find, together with how many individuals or colonies of animals you saw. You could include a note on whether they were in a rockpool, on a rock, stranded or in the sand, make sketches of your finds and stick in any useful photographs. You can also buy a waterproof notebook or an underwater slate so that you can make notes while you are on the shore about any interesting animal behaviour you observe. All of this information is extremely useful for building up a picture of your local shores. You can note how the life changes with the seasons, and also from beach to beach. By contributing your records, you can help to further marine science and information on how to do this is given on page 212.

Date and time:
Location:
O.S.Grid reference/GPS reading:
Weather:
Height of tide:
Sea state:
Pollution: e.g. oil, sewage, litter
Brief description of the shore:
List of species:
Number of individuals:
Habitat:
Any additional features:

Seashore Safaris

# 2. Living between the tides

**The narrow area lying between the highest and lowest tide marks on the shore is called the intertidal or littoral zone. This area can shelter an astonishing diversity of plant and animal life living between the tides, both on rocky and sandy shores.**

There are four main types of shore found in Britain and Ireland – rock, sand, mud and shingle.

Each has its own characteristic flora and fauna, and no two shores around our coasts are exactly the same.

Rocky or sandy shores can be found all around the coast of Britain and Ireland. Approximately 34% of the coastline comprises rocky shores and about 25% sandy beaches.

'Seashore Safaris' concentrates on rocky and sandy shores and their associated wildlife. This section gives background information on tides, types of shore, factors affecting life on the shore, adaptations for survival and food chains and food webs.

**Forces shaping the shore** 20
**Rocky and sandy shores** 22
**Survival on the shore** 24

# 2 Living between the tides

## 2. Living between the tides

# Forces shaping the shore

**Inhabitants of the shore have to be able to survive rapidly changing environmental conditions. Waves, tides, currents, salinity, temperature, light intensity and availability, degree of exposure and other factors all determine the distribution of the flora and fauna present on a rocky or sandy shore.**

Even though the physical living conditions between the tides are harsh, most shores support a wide variety and number of species, due to the variety of micro-habitats present. Some of the main factors determining the type of shore found are outlined here.

### Tides and tidal ranges

Most of our shores are subject to a twice daily cycle of **ebb** (going out) and **flow** (coming in) of the tides. In UK waters, high tides occur approximately every 12 hours 25 minutes.

Tides are the main factor controlling life on the shore, and have a considerable influence. They are produced by the gravitational pull of the moon and sun on the earth. **Spring tides** occur throughout the year when the moon and sun work together, every two weeks at the times of new and full moon. These produce the lowest low tides and the highest high tides. The largest spring tides of all (when the maximum shore is exposed) occur around 21st March and 23rd September each year at the time of the equinoxes when the sun and moon are exactly aligned. These are called **equinoctial spring tides**.

In between the spring tides, **neap tides** occur when the moon and sun work against each other. This is just after the time when the moon is in its first and third quarter. Neap tides produce the highest low tides and the lowest high tides.

The tidal range is the vertical distance between high and low tide levels. The Bristol Channel has the second highest tidal range in the world. At Weston-Super-Mare, the range is over 11 m mean spring tide, while the extreme range at Avonmouth is just over 15 m. Neaps in south west Scotland may be less than 1m. The north-east coast of Ireland has an average spring tide of 1m and a neap tidal range of only 0.5 m. The south coast of the UK, such as Dorset, experiences a range of only 2 m. The world's largest tidal range occurs jointly in the Bay of Fundy in Eastern Canada, and in Ungava Bay on the northern coast of Quebec, where the sea level can change by up to 17 m during the day.

Local geology determines the type of shore formed

## Geology

The geology or rock structure of our coastline varies enormously from high rugged cliffs and limestone pavements to sweeping sandy beaches. The type of shore formed depends on the local underlying rock type and structure. Each coastline is unique in terms of hardness and resistance to wave action. Rock type also influences the slope and topography of the shore and in turn, determines the area available for intertidal species to colonise. Barnacles and limpets are successful on steep shores, while mussels and seaweeds are more common on gently-sloping or horizontal shores.

## Exposure

Exposure refers to the amount of wave action or tidal currents. The type of shore found is determined by the amount of wave action. This in turn determines what plant and animal communities occur. An eroding shore is a rocky shore found in areas with fairly heavy surf.

A depositing shore is a sandy shore, formed from particles deposited by waves and water currents and is found in more sheltered areas. There are **sheltered** and **exposed** rocky and sandy shores. This refers to the degree of wind and wave action to which a shore is exposed. There are also moderately exposed shores in between and these are the most common type found around the UK. They support a greater variety of habitats.

Sheltered rocky shores usually have some protection such as a headland. The rocks here are often hidden by a dense covering of brown seaweeds. Sheltered shores provide the best areas for studying zonation.

Exposed rocky shores are subjected to constant wave action and occur on the open coast. They cannot support a dense growth of algae, and are dominated by animals such as barnacles and mussels.

On a sandy shore, wave action determines the size of particles that make up the shore. These vary from coarse sand or fine damp sands on exposed shores to coarse, clean, well drained sands on less-exposed shores, and fine muds and silt on the most sheltered shores and in estuaries. The size of sediment particles influences what can actually live in or on it.

## 2. Living between the tides

# Rocky and sandy shores

**Rocky and sandy shores are located around our coasts and are very different and rewarding environments to explore as they are often easily accessible for visiting and studying. Throughout the year there is always something of interest on our shores.**

Rocky shores are termed **eroding shores** as they are found where wave action wears away softer rocks, leaving harder rocks exposed. Their character depends on the underlying geology and the amount of wave exposure. Rocky shores can consist of rock platforms, rock ledges, rocky reefs or areas of boulders and they are the most variable coastal habitat in the UK. All of these factors are important in determining what plant and animal species will be found in this dynamic environment.

Sandy beaches are termed **depositing shores**. They are much less steep than rocky shores and this allows sand to accumulate. They are formed from small rock particles, mainly silica, which have been eroded and shaped by wind and wave action and then deposited. If you pick up a handful of sand and look at it through a magnifying glass or hand lens, you will discover that the grains are many different sizes. This is an important factor in determining the type, abundance and distribution of animal life on a sandy shore. At low tide, these wide expanses of sand may appear empty and lifeless but there is plenty of life waiting to be discovered, especially on protected, sheltered beaches where the sand is finer and more stable. Exposed sandy shores will have less animal life, due to disturbance caused by wave action. Intertidal sand can be a difficult place to live, as there are no surfaces such as boulders or seaweeds in which animals can shelter. Most life here has to be able to burrow in order to survive. The amount of water in the sand determines how well animals can burrow. However some molluscs and crustaceans may excavate shafts or tunnels, ready to escape. Certain bristleworms, live in tubes. These tubes are produced by the animals themselves and may be adorned with sand and shell fragments.

**Page 23:** top, example of a rocky shore and below, example of a sandy shore.

## 2. Living between the tides

# Survival on the shore

**Life is tough for organisms living between the tides on the shore, as they are often uncovered by the tide and exposed to the elements twice a day, and then covered by the sea again hours later.**

The higher up the shore an organism lives, the more tolerant it is to exposure and the drying effects of air and temperature fluctuations. On more sheltered shores, the risk of being washed away by wave action is decreased, and so more fragile species can be found. Some of the most important factors that affect the survival of shore flora and fauna are: **dessication**, temperature extremes, salinity, wave action, oxygen, light, predation, competition, trampling, pollution and climate change.

### Survival tactics

Even in such a dynamic environment life thrives, and **intertidal** species have adopted some interesting survival strategies, especially at low tide. Some of these tactics include:

- having thicker or flatter shells to withstand wave action on exposed shores
- living in areas where there is still water at low tide, e.g. rockpools or crevices
- adopting methods of camouflage
- using strong suction pads to clamp down on rocks, to avoid being washed away
- using a plate or door (**operculum**) to keep water in at low tide
- closing both shell valves at low tide
- having a long thin body covered with a layer of slime
- having different shapes on different parts of the shore
- burrowing into sand or mud

### Eat or be eaten

As in any environment, the shore inhabitants have to eat to survive, or risk being eaten themselves. Marine algae are called **producers** and make their own food using energy from the sun. Animals are termed **consumers** as they have to gain their energy by eating plants or other animals. There are three types of consumers. **Herbivores**, such as limpets and periwinkles only eat plants. **Carnivores**, including starfish, eat other animals. **Omnivores**, such as sea urchins, eat both plants and animals. Each organism living on the shore will be a link or connection in a **food chain**. Each food chain will have a plant as the first link such as **phytoplankton** or seaweed. There may be hundreds of separate intertidal food chains, and these combined, form a complex **food web**.

## PROJECT:

Study the rocky shore food web below to see how many separate food chains you can spot. One example has been completed for you (right). You could also try to construct your own food chains and food webs, based on your shore observations. Remember, all food chains and webs start with plants!

### Example of a food chain

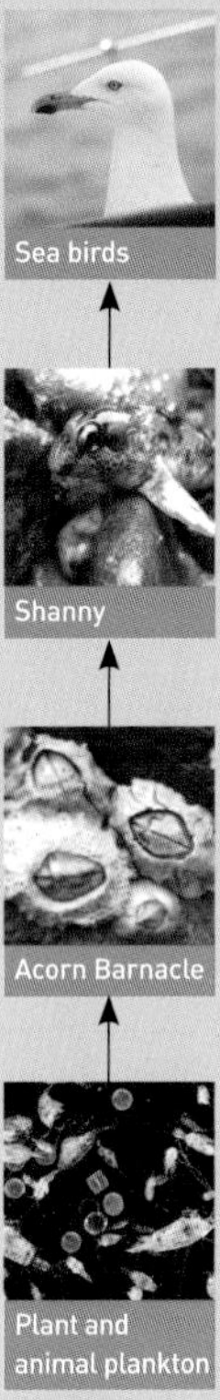

Sea birds

Shanny

Acorn Barnacle

Plant and animal plankton

### Example of a food web

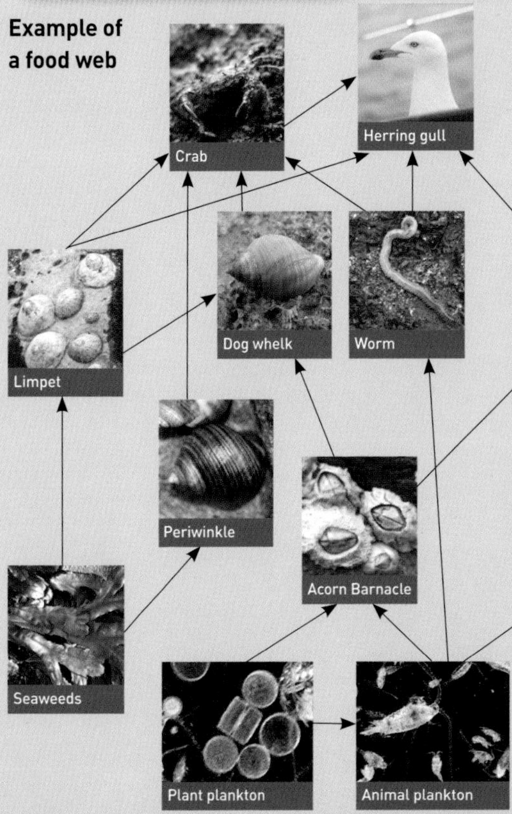

Crab

Herring gull

Dog whelk

Worm

Limpet

Shanny

Periwinkle

Acorn Barnacle

Common prawn

Seaweeds

Plant plankton

Animal plankton

Seashore Safaris

# 3. Zonation

**Plants and animals are not distributed haphazardly over a shore, but are arranged according to a pattern termed zonation.**

**On a rocky shore, the constant twice daily rise and fall of the tide often produces a number of distinct bands or zones, which can be recognised by characteristic plants and animals.**

These bands can be divided into the splash zone (**supralittoral fringe** page 30) at the landward end of the shore, upper shore (**upper eulittoral** page 32) middle shore (**eulittoral** page 34) and lower shore (**sublittoral fringe** page 36) found at the seaward end.

This pattern of biological zones can sometimes be seen around the coast as coloured stripes and is often best observed on sheltered rocky shores. The zones are formed where certain organisms are most dominant and are determined by how long the shore is covered and uncovered by the sea as the tide goes in and out, and in turn how long it is exposed to the wind and the sun. When you learn to recognize the key indicator species of each zone, you will be able to establish what part of the shore you are observing. However, there will be some overlap between each zone, and it may take some practice to do this. Species of brown seaweed have a particular pattern of zonation along the shore and this is illustrated on page 187. The higher up the shore a species lives, the more adapted it is. The lower shore is the best place to live as a truly marine creature. Here however, there may be strong competition for food and space.

**Compared with rocky shores, sandy shore zonation is not so clearly defined and is constantly changing due to the shifting nature of sand grains.** It will depend on local environmental conditions. Organisms are distributed down the shore according to their ability to withstand extended periods out of water as well as associated extremes in temperature. The sand of the upper shore area remains drier for longer periods than that on the lower shore. Several species of tubeworms occur on the middle shore. However, most life is found on the lower shore where the sand is much wetter. Here the sand only dries out on the surface during low tide. There is also vertical zonation within the sand created by the amount of oxygen available (which decreases with depth), and the size of sand particles. As you walk down the shore from the strandline to the water's edge, the type and variety of inhabitants, together with the nature of the beach, changes progressively.


| | |
|---|---|
| **Rocky shore zonation** | **28** |
| **Splash zone** | **30** |
| **Upper shore** | **32** |
| **Middle shore** | **34** |
| **Lower shore** | **36** |
| **Laminarian zone** | **38** |
| **Sandy shore zonation** | **40** |

Sandy shore

Rocky shore

3. Zonation | Rocky shore

# Rocky shore zonation

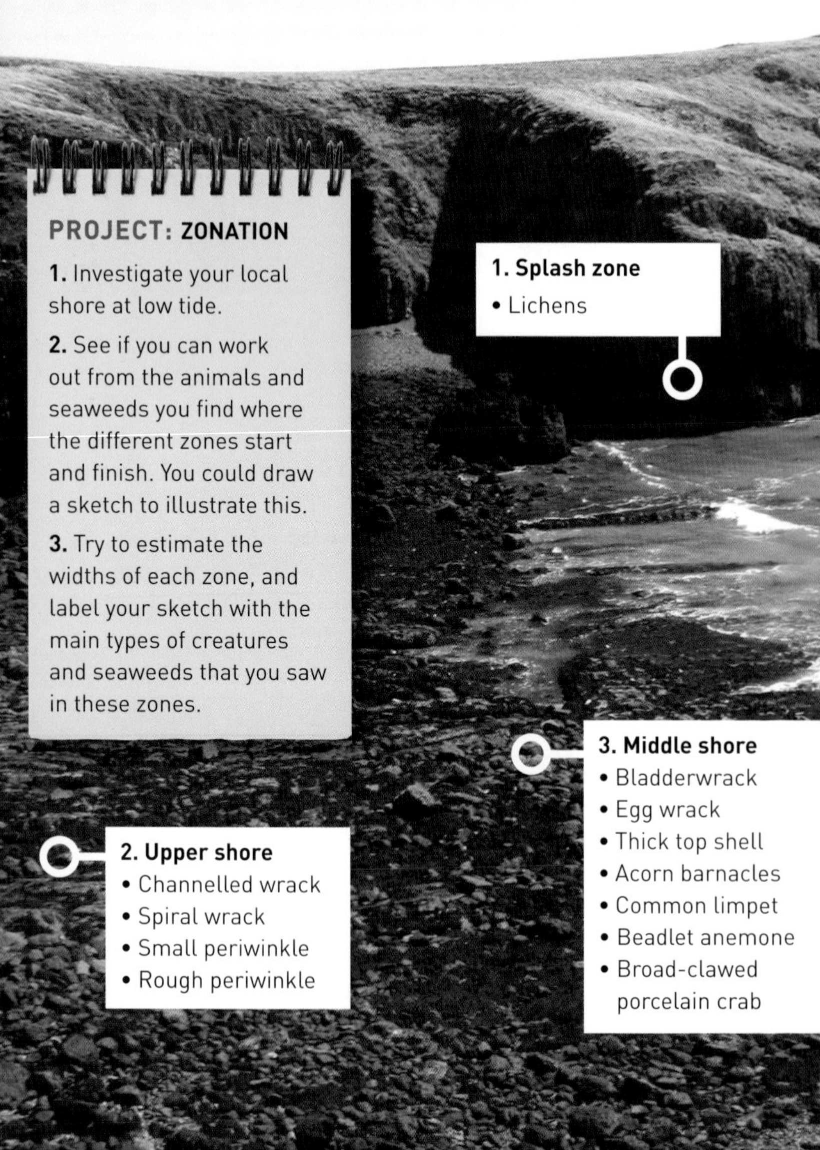

**PROJECT: ZONATION**

**1.** Investigate your local shore at low tide.

**2.** See if you can work out from the animals and seaweeds you find where the different zones start and finish. You could draw a sketch to illustrate this.

**3.** Try to estimate the widths of each zone, and label your sketch with the main types of creatures and seaweeds that you saw in these zones.

**1. Splash zone**

- Lichens

**2. Upper shore**

- Channelled wrack
- Spiral wrack
- Small periwinkle
- Rough periwinkle

**3. Middle shore**

- Bladderwrack
- Egg wrack
- Thick top shell
- Acorn barnacles
- Common limpet
- Beadlet anemone
- Broad-clawed porcelain crab

5. Laminarian zone
• Kelps
• Common urchin
4. Lower shore
• Serrated wrack
• Thongweed
• Red seaweeds
• Green sea urchins
• Cushionstar
• Worm pipefish
• Dead man's fingers
• Painted top shell

# Splash zone

**The splash zone is the area at the top of the shore with limited contact with the sea.**

It is mainly salt spray that affects life here. This area is exposed to the sun and to the drying effects of the wind. Rocks are bare, apart from patches of colourful **lichens**. Lichens are made up of a fungus and an alga living together, and occur in many forms.

They are a link between the seaweeds of the rocky shore and the flowering plants of the cliffs. The common seashore lichens described here occur in vertical zones. Grey lichens (sea ivory and crab's eye lichen) are found at the top, orange lichens next, followed by black lichens such as black tar lichen, which extend to the upper shore.

## 1. Black tar lichen

*Verrucaria maura*

This smooth, encrusting lichen may cover large areas of the splash zone, just below the band of orange lichens. It may be mistaken for a patch of dried oil or paint, but is in fact a living organism.

## 2. Yellow lichen

*Xanthoria parietina*

This yellow/orange lichen forms a band along the rocks above high tide level and occurs just below Sea ivory.

## 3. Sea ivory

*Ramalina siliquosa*

This greenish-grey lichen has stiff upright branches up to 5 cm long. The disc-shaped reproductive (fruiting) bodies near the tip are white or pale brown.

## 4. Crab's eye lichen

*Ochrelechia parella*

Forms rounded patches on rocks, 3 – 10 cm in diameter. It has grey saucer-shaped fruiting bodies.

## 5. A lichen

*Lichina pygmaea*

This lichen forms tufts of branching, flattened lobes up to 15 mm long. It is dark brownish black and can sometimes be mistaken for the small red seaweed *Catenella caespitosa* (p.199). It occurs on open, exposed rock faces near high water mark of neap tides.

# Upper shore

**The upper shore is the zone above the mean high water mark. This is only covered during high spring tides, and is dominated by a few seaweeds and animals which hide in rock crevices, and graze on the rocks.**

Species found here can tolerate the extreme physical conditions prevailing for most of the time. The greatest danger to animals here is drying out or dessication, and they have to withstand long periods of exposure.

The number of species living on the upper shore is small, but there may be many individuals.

Animals living here tend to have a protective outer shell or are permanently attached to the rock surface.

A common indicator of this zone is the brown seaweed **channelled wrack (1)**. It is covered with water for only a few hours once a fortnight. **Spiral wrack (2)** grows in a band below channelled wrack, especially on sheltered shores. The **rough periwinkle (4)** is adapted to life here as it has a type of lung that allows it to breathe air. **Acorn barnacles (5)** dominate the rock surfaces. Look in dead acorn barnacle shells with a hand lens for the tiny **small periwinkle (6)**.

### DID YOU KNOW?

The upper shore is only covered by the sea for about 20% of the time.

## TRY SEARCHING FOR

1. **Channelled wrack**
   *Pelvetia canaliculata* (p.193)
2. **Spiral wrack**
   *Fucus spiralis* (p.192)
3. **Gutweed**
   *Ulva intestinalis* (p.189)
4. **Rough periwinkle**
   *Littorina saxatilis* (p.131)
5. **Acorn barnacle**
   (p.107)
6. **Small periwinkle**
   *Melarhaphe neritoides* (p.131)

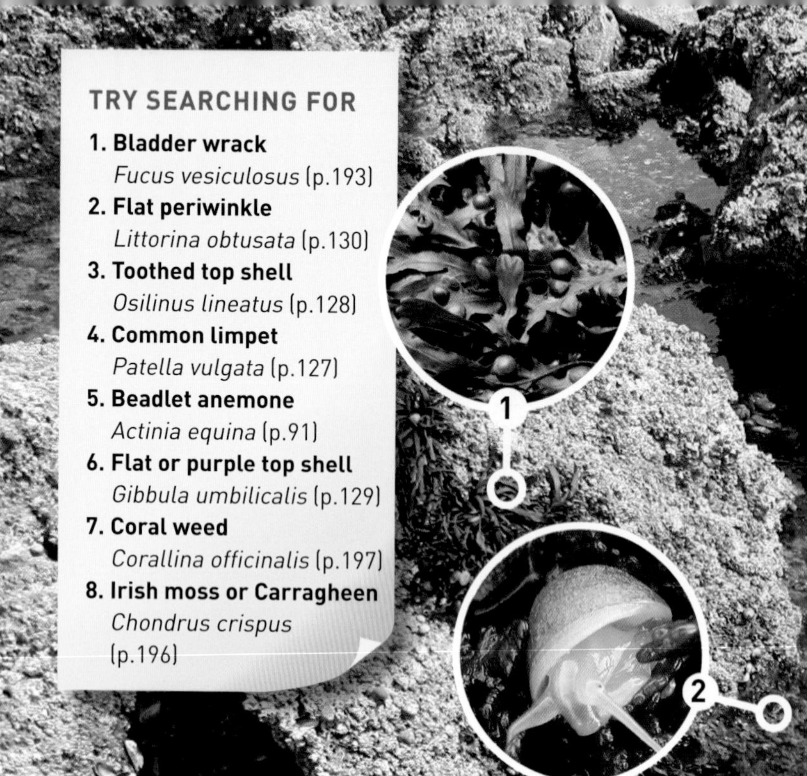


## 3. Zonation | Rocky shore

# Middle shore

**The middle shore is the zone between mean high water and mean low water. This area of the shore is subjected to daily covering and uncovering by both spring and neap tides, and is usually the widest area of the shore that is exposed.**

The area is dominated by types of brown seaweed called wracks such as **bladder wrack (1)**, and animals called **periwinkles (2)** and **top shells (3 and 6).** On the **middle shore** there is a greater diversity of species than on the upper shore, and these species can be classed as true shore dwellers.

The key to survival here is to stay as wet as possible, to avoid predators, and to be able to withstand wave action. When the tide is out, many animals seek shelter in damp crevices, overhangs and underneath seaweeds. The middle shore is covered by seawater for 20 – 80% of the time.

## YOU MAY ALSO FIND

- Egg wrack (p.192)
- False Irish moss (p.198)
- Pepper dulse (p.196)
- Common or Edible periwinkle (p.130)
- Dog whelk (p.132)
- Barnacles (p.106)
- Common mussel (p.143)
- Broad-clawed porcelain crab (p.114)
- Common shore crab (p.114)
- Breadcrumb sponge (p.80)

## 3. Zonation | Rocky shore

# Lower shore

**This is the zone below mean low water. It is accessible only at the lowest tides and is often the most rewarding area to investigate.**

Creatures here cannot tolerate prolonged exposure to air. The lowest areas are uncovered for only a short period during a few days of spring tides every fortnight. The lower shore is most prolific, in terms of species diversity, but there may be strong competition for food and space.

Plants and animals here are fully or nearly marine. **Serrated wrack (1)** and red seaweeds such as **dulse (2)** are indicators of this area. They provide extra food and cover for animals. At very low spring tides, kelp forests are uncovered just off-shore in the sub-littoral fringe or Laminarian zone (page 38).

The lower shore is covered by the sea for approximately 80–100% of the time.

### TRY SEARCHING FOR

1. **Toothed or Serrated wrack**
   *Fucus serratus* (p.192)
2. **Dulse**
   *Palmaria palmata* (p.199)
3. **Shore clingfish**
   *Lepadogaster lepadogaster* (p.173)
4. **Breadcrumb sponge**
   *Halichondria panicea* (p.80)
5. **Green or Shore sea urchin**
   *Psammechinus miliaris* (p.162)
6. **Sea slug**
   *Facelina auriculata* (p.138)
7. **Snakelocks anemone**
   *Anemonia viridis* (p.90)
8. **Edible or Brown crab**
   *Cancer pagurus* (p.113)

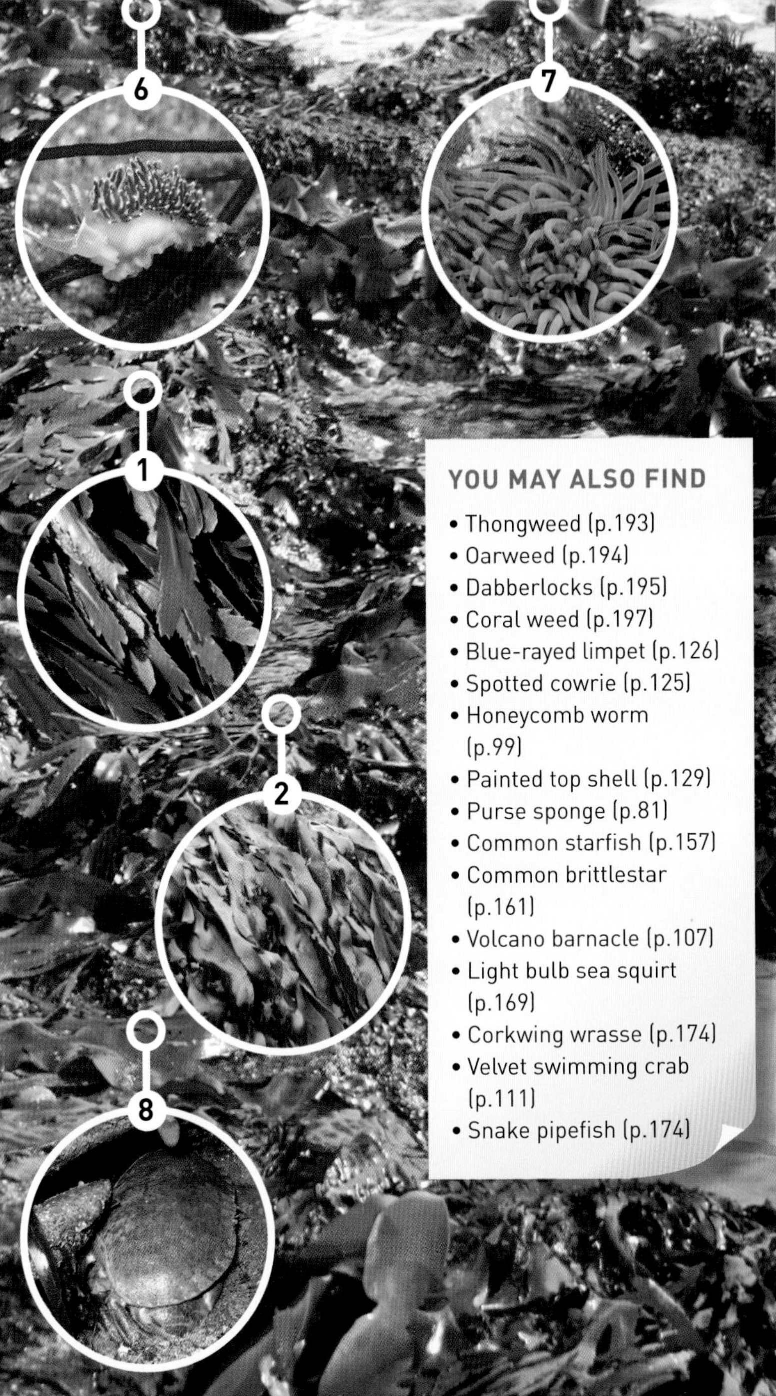


## YOU MAY ALSO FIND

- Thongweed (p.193)
- Oarweed (p.194)
- Dabberlocks (p.195)
- Coral weed (p.197)
- Blue-rayed limpet (p.126)
- Spotted cowrie (p.125)
- Honeycomb worm (p.99)
- Painted top shell (p.129)
- Purse sponge (p.81)
- Common starfish (p.157)
- Common brittlestar (p.161)
- Volcano barnacle (p.107)
- Light bulb sea squirt (p.169)
- Corkwing wrasse (p.174)
- Velvet swimming crab (p.111)
- Snake pipefish (p.174)

## 3. Zonation | Rocky shore

# Laminarian zone

**Laminarians or kelps are large brown algae, only exposed at very low spring tides, with the greatest extents uncovered twice a year during equinoctial spring tides.**

These marine algae often form kelp forests (see background image), and are found below the low tide level in the **sub-littoral zone**. The seaweed is attached firmly to a rock by a branched 'root-like' holdfast. This provides shelter for a variety of animals such as brittlestars, sea squirts, and small crabs.

The stem or stipe may be rough or smooth, and provides a surface to which other seaweeds and animals may attach. The frond or blade is branched or strap-like, and encrusting colonial animals such as hydroids or bryozoans may live on it. Kelps are grazed by the Blue-rayed limpet and the Common sea urchin. Some kelp species are used as health foods and supplements.

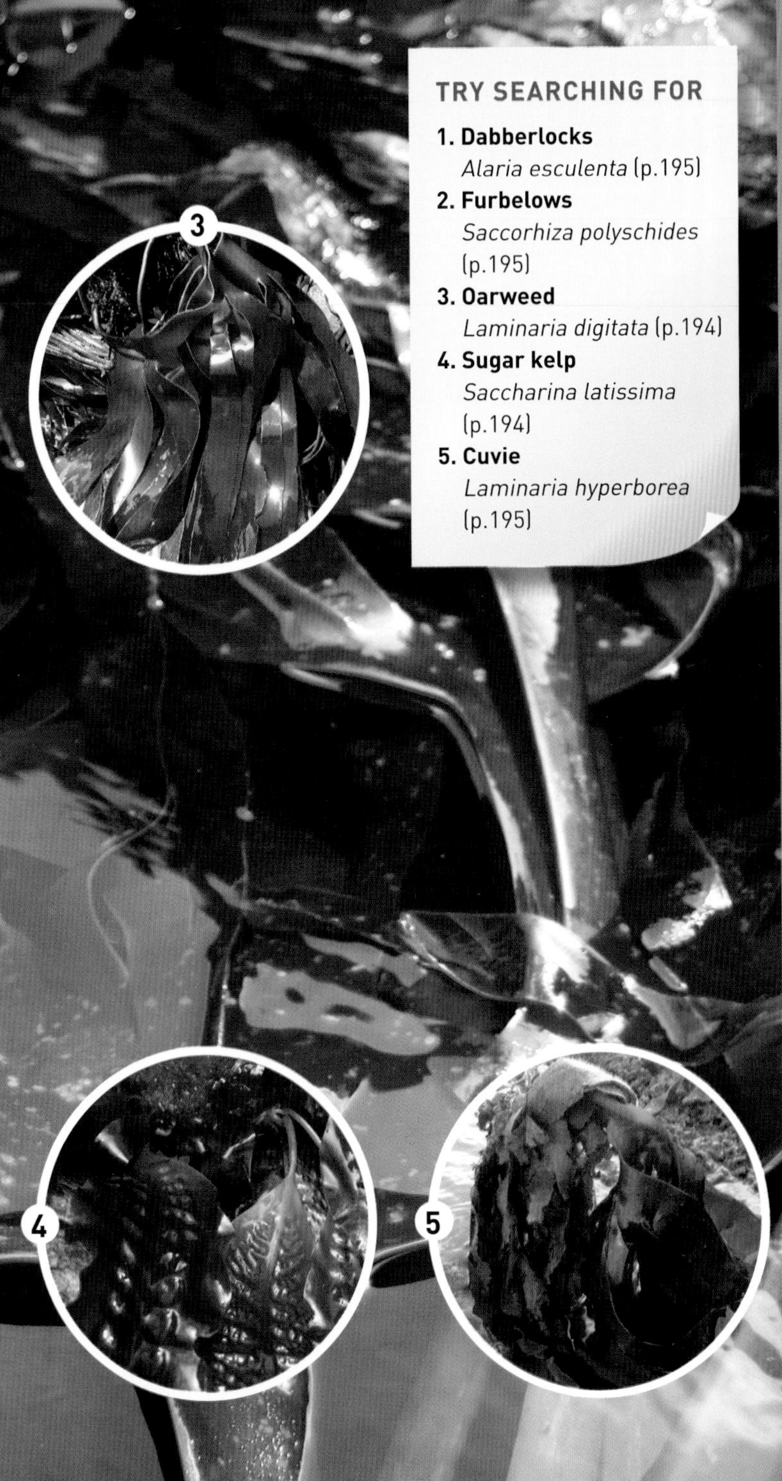


## TRY SEARCHING FOR

1. **Dabberlocks**
   *Alaria esculenta* (p.195)
2. **Furbelows**
   *Saccorhiza polyschides* (p.195)
3. **Oarweed**
   *Laminaria digitata* (p.194)
4. **Sugar kelp**
   *Saccharina latissima* (p.194)
5. **Cuvie**
   *Laminaria hyperborea* (p.195)

# Sandy shore zonation

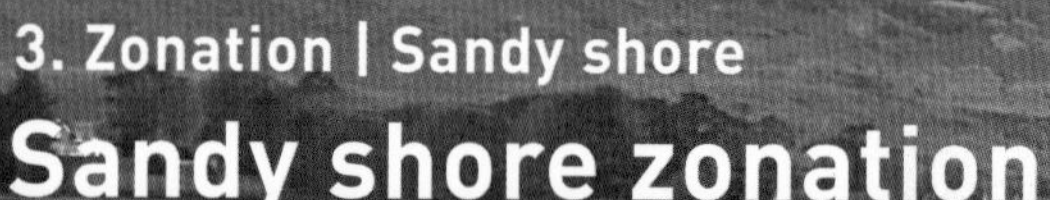

**Upper shore and strandline**

- Sandhopper
- Strandline beetle
- Sea slater

**PROJECT:**

**1.** On sandy shores, you can try to collect some common **epifauna** from the sand surface and **infauna** from within the sediment (e.g. bivalves or bristle worms) to observe what adaptation these animals exhibit to overcoming the difficulties of living on the sand surface and within the sand respectively.

**2.** You could draw them and label them in your field notebook.

**3.** Remember to follow the Seashore Code (page 15).

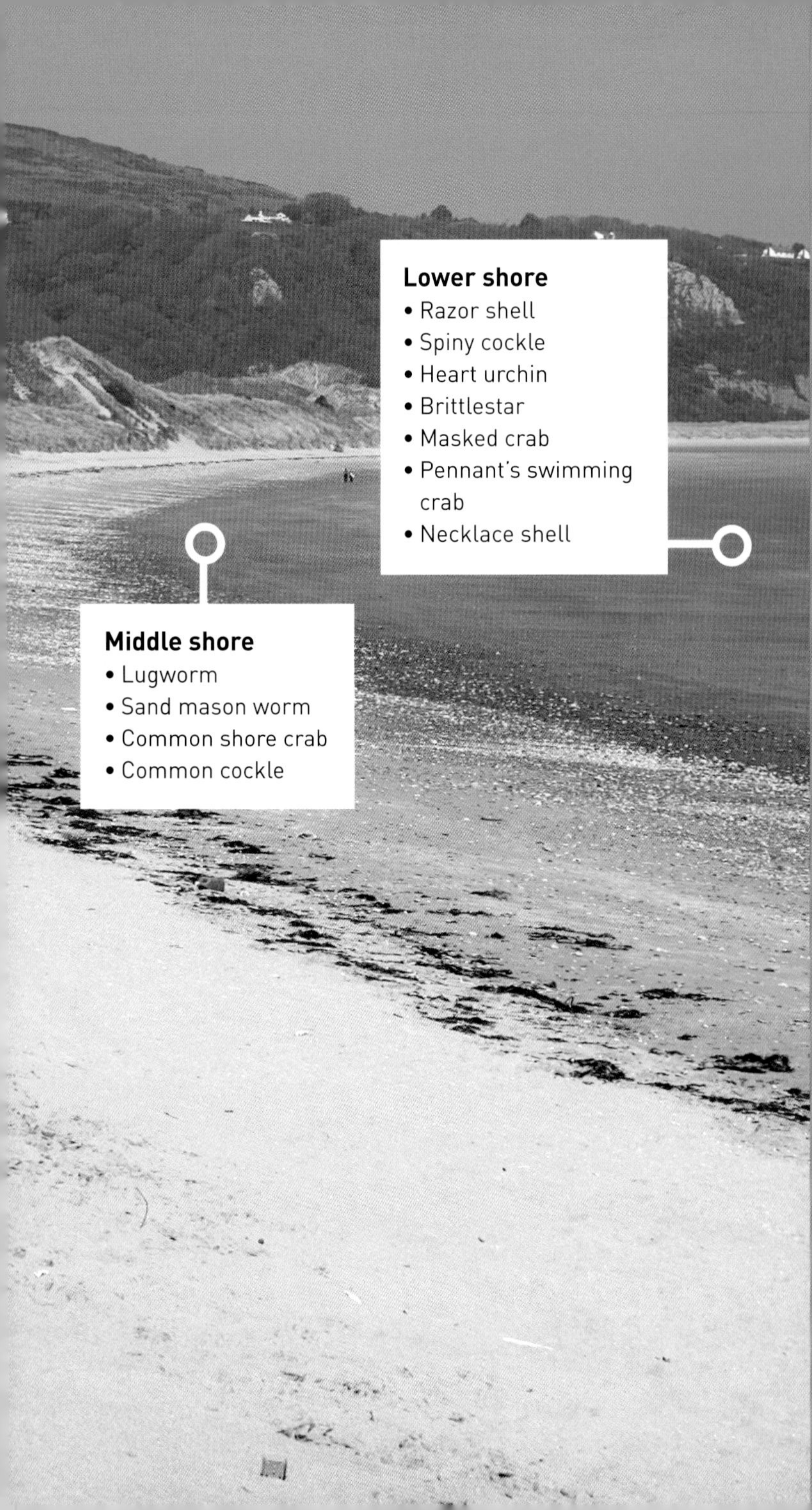

**Lower shore**
- Razor shell
- Spiny cockle
- Heart urchin
- Brittlestar
- Masked crab
- Pennant's swimming crab
- Necklace shell

**Middle shore**
- Lugworm
- Sand mason worm
- Common shore crab
- Common cockle

## Seashore Safaris

# 4. Habitats

**Both rocky and sandy shores have particular habitats available to the many creatures living on them. However, they are very different environments.** The rocky shore is a very complex and dynamic habitat. Depending on the structure of the shore, there may be additional micro-habitats present which increase available living space, and in turn the number of species present.

These **micro-habitats** may include rockpools, surge gullies, crevices and boulders. The conditions provided by these areas pose their own survival challenges for the plants and animals living there. Sheltering or living in cracks or under boulders and overhangs is the only way many delicate or soft-bodied species survive, and other less common species can also take refuge here. The wealth of wildlife that exists under and on rocks, under seaweeds and in rockpools is astounding, and this abundance is found in no other shore environment.

As a habitat, intertidal sand can be a desperate place to live as there are no places to hide from predators, and low tide exposes creatures to the effects of the wind and sun. The sand surface is constantly shifting, but a few centimetres down, conditions are more stable. When the tide comes in, the effects of wave action also have to be overcome. This means that on a sandy shore, it is critical that the inhabitants are able to burrow into the sand to escape these effects. Compared with a rocky shore, the number of habitats available on a sandy shore is small, and creatures are found living in four main areas. These are in and on the sand, in sandy pools and on the strandline.

When you know where to look for hidden wildlife on our seashores, you will be amazed at what you can find.


**Crevices** 44
**Surge gullies** 46
**Overhangs** 48
**Rockpools** 50
**On and under seaweed** 52
**On boulders** 54
**Under boulders** 56
**Strandline** 58
**In and on sand** 60
**In pools and on the strandline** 62
**Signs of life and quiz** 64

4 | Habitats

# Crevices

**Crevices, cracks and fissures can make a considerable difference to the chances of survival of shore species. They stay cool, dark and damp longer than exposed rock, and provide much needed shelter, shade and a safe refuge from large predators.**

Deeper crevices may house specialized communities. Seaweed and animals often congregate in small cracks and crevices on the rock surface, especially on exposed shores, as they offer some protection from wave action. Many mobile animals such as worms, squat lobsters, sea cucumbers, periwinkles, dog whelks and fish use crevices as refuges, moving in and out with the tide to feed. Other inhabitants feed on organic matter which accumulates within the crevice.

Barnacles extend their feeding legs beyond the crevice entrance, to trap suspended particles in the water current. Beadlet, gem and daisy anemones use crevices as a permanent living space, and sea slugs such as sea lemons **(2a)**, may lay their eggs in them **(2b)**.

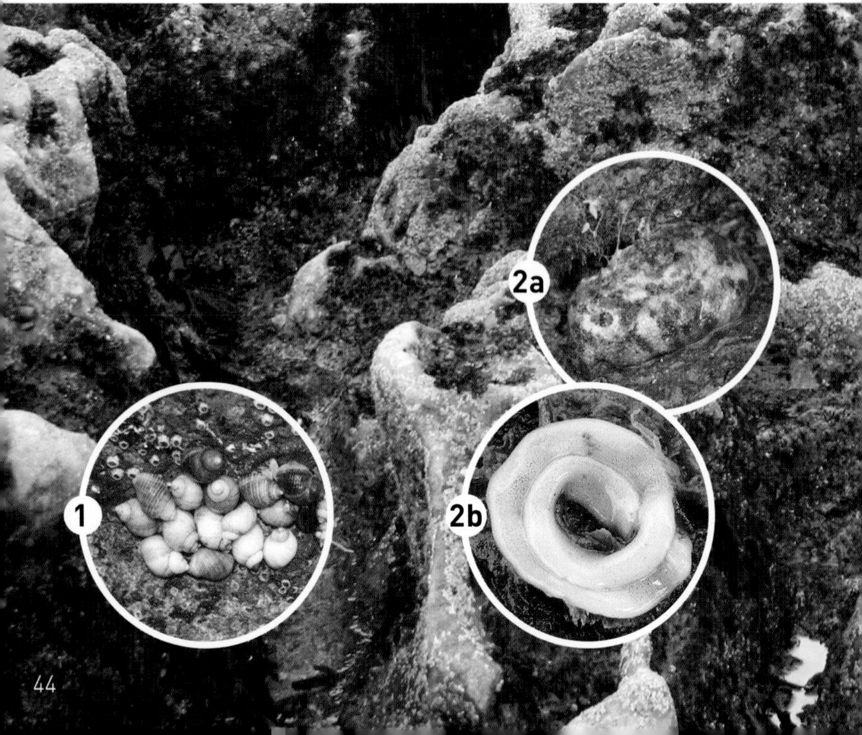

## TRY SEARCHING FOR

1. **Dog whelks**
   *Nucella lapillus* (p.132)

2a / 2b. **Sea lemon and eggs**
   *Archidoris pseudoargus* (p.139)

3. **Spiny starfish**
   *Marthasterias glacialis* (p.159)
4. **Shanny**
   *Lipophrys pholis* (p.177)
5. **Gem anemone**
   *Aulactinia verrucosa* (p.89)
6. **Squat lobster (juvenile)**
   *Galathea strigosa*
7. **Rough periwinkle**
   *Littorina saxatilis* (p.131)

## 4. Habitats | Rocky shore

# Surge gullies

**Gullies may follow fault lines or bedding planes in the underlying rock and run straight out to sea. This habitat can extend the range of offshore creatures closer to the shore.**

Water surges in and out of rocky gullies, and the strength of these tidal streams and exposure to wave action influences the types of species able to live here. Waves surging through rocky gullies bring much needed food carried in suspension. Mobile sediment is often trapped at the base of gullies. Large groups of the dahlia anemone can be found living here.

Other mobile visitors include the edible crab and common starfish.

Beds of common mussels thrive at the base of surge gullies. Groups of common starfish can be found feeding on them **(3)**.

The rocky walls of surge gullies support rich invertebrate communities such as sponges, sea squirts, hydroids and anemones.

The elegant anemone occurs in many colour forms, and is especially common in rocky gullies.

## TRY SEARCHING FOR

1. **Dahlia anemone** *Urticina felina* (p.83)
2. **Elegant anemone** *Sagartia elegans* (p.91)
3. **Common starfish** *Asterias rubens* (p.157) feeding on common mussels *Mytilus edulis* (p.143)
4. **Baked bean sea squirt** *Dendrodoa grossularia* (p.169)
5. **Breadcrumb sponge** *Halichondria panicea* (p.80)
6. **Purse sponge** *Grantia compressa* (p.81)
7. **Edible crab** *Cancer pagurus* (p.113)
8. **Common mussel** *Mytilus edulis* (p.143)

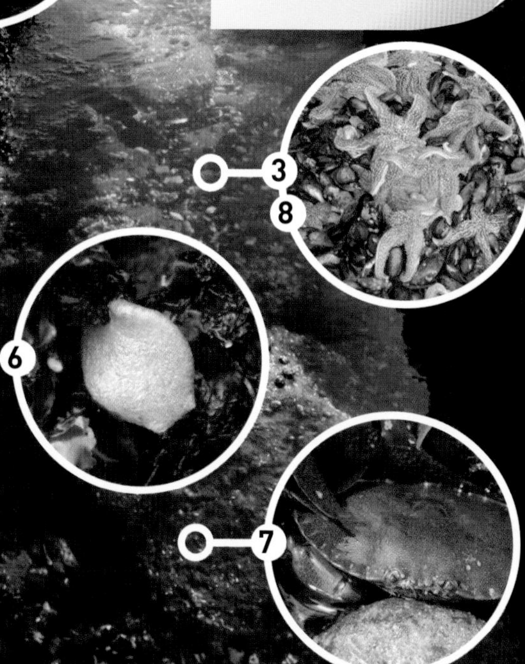

Observing the soft coral Dead man's fingers under an overhang

## 4. Habitats | Rocky shore

# Overhangs

**Overhanging rocks are important on the shore, as they provide shade and shelter from the sun and waves. Large rock overhangs are like mini-caves, as there may be a lack of light.**

Seaweeds are rarely found, due to the low light levels, but the sides and roofs of overhangs can support a rich variety of animal life such as sea squirts, hydroids, sea mats, sponges, soft corals and sea anemones. You may be lucky enough to spot the brightly coloured Devonshire cup coral or the scarlet and gold star coral. The amount of wave action, sea spray and available light determines the unique communities found under overhangs on different parts of the shore.

## TRY SEARCHING FOR

1. **Beadlet anemone**
   *Actinia equina* (p.91)
2. **Breadcrumb sponge**
   *Halichondria panicea* (p.80)
3. **Volcano Barnacle**
   *Balanus perforatus* (p.107)
4. **Hydroids** (p.84)
5. **Dog whelks and eggs**
   *Nucella lapillus* (p.132)
6. **Dead man's fingers**
   *Alcyonium digitatum* (p.87)
7. **Jewel anemone**
   *Corynactis viridis*

## YOU MAY ALSO FIND

- **Common mussels** (p.143)
- **Spotted cowrie** (p.125)
- **Scarlet and gold star coral** (p.86)
- **Devonshire cup coral** (p.87)

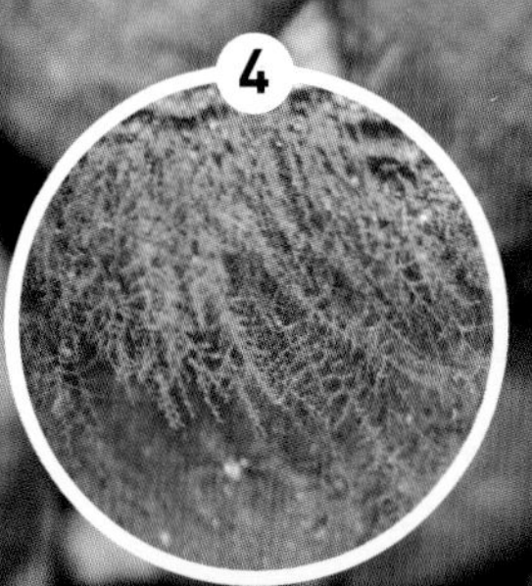

## 4. Habitats | Rocky shore

# Rockpools

**Rockpools are among the most interesting of shore micro-habitats. They vary from small, shallow depressions to large, deep pools suitable for snorkelling, and can be found from the upper to the lower shore. They form where the geology of the shore allows seawater to collect in hollows in the bedrock when the tide retreats. Rockpools at different heights on the shore will have different inhabitants.**

A rockpool is like a natural marine 'aquarium' and offers a free, educational resource for anyone to observe marine life in the wild. Not all rockpool life will be visible at first, but if you approach a rockpool slowly and quietly, and sit at the edge keeping still and silent, you will soon see many creatures going about their everyday lives in front of you. Avoid putting your reflection on the water surface though, as this will frighten some creatures away. Rockpools offer the best survival chances for animals and seaweeds that need to be submerged all the time. However, they are not necessarily a refuge for creatures stranded by low tide.

Life can be difficult in a rockpool, and conditions in pools can vary greatly between high and low tides, depending on their location on the shore. Those on the upper shore are subjected to freshwater run-off from the land, and wide temperature ranges, allowing the green seaweed gutweed to dominate. Shallow middle shore pools are characterized by coral weed, and deeper pools on the lower shore allow large brown seaweeds such as serrated wrack or kelp species to thrive. The more time you spend looking into a rockpool, the more you will see.

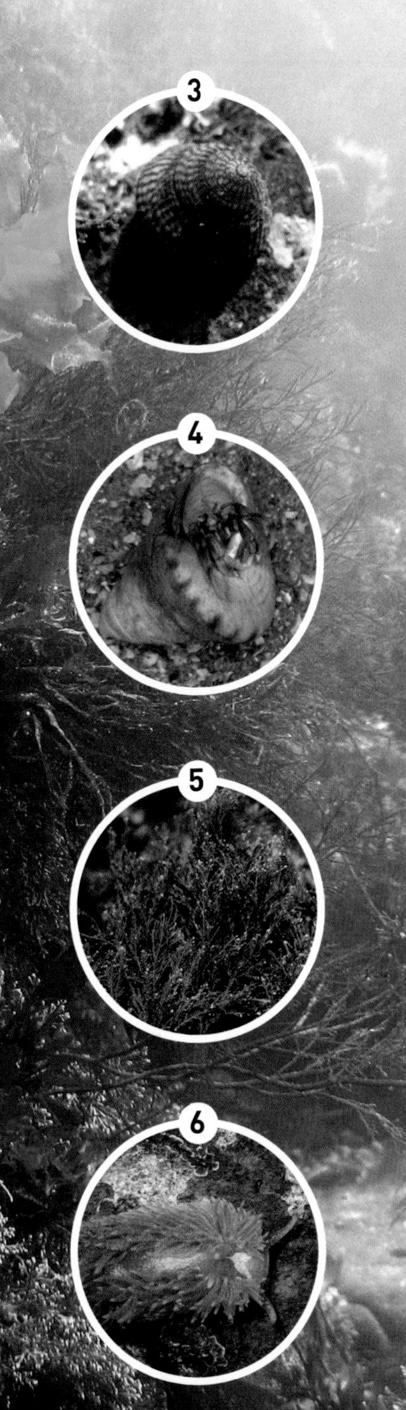


## TRY SEARCHING FOR

1. **Connemara clingfish**
   *Lepadogaster candolii*
2. **Sea lettuce**
   *Ulva lactuca* (p.188)
3. **Grey top shell**
   *Gibbula cineraria* (p.128)
4. **Common hermit crab**
   *Pagarus bernhardus* (p.113)
5. **Coral weed**
   *Corallina officinalis* (p.197)
6. **Grey sea slug**
   *Aeolidia papillosa* (p.138)

## YOU MAY ALSO FIND

- **Snakelocks anemone** (p.90)
- **Common prawn** (p.116)
- **Irish moss** (p.196)
- **Sea oak** (p.191)

## PROJECT: ROCKPOOLS

**1.** Visit the rocky shore at night with an adult . Take a torch and investigate the micro-habitats. You may see many creatures not normally seen during the day, feeding at night.
**2.** Choose a rockpool on your local shore and draw a sketch of it. Try and map where you find each creature and seaweed within the pool and surrounding it. Label all the micro-habitats you can see.

4. Habitats | Rocky shore

# On and under seaweed

**Many shore species shelter amongst the dampness of hanging seaweeds when the tide is out.**

These include sea snails, crabs and fish. The fronds of brown seaweeds are often home to groups of animals forming colonies such as hydroids **(4)** or sea firs, and bryozoans **(5)** or sea mats. Kelp holdfasts (p.186) provide food and shelter for a variety of marine life. The holdfast may be colonized by attached and encrusting organisms such as sea squirts and hydroids, and other animals such as brittlestars and worms shelter within the holdfast itself.

The fronds and stipes of seaweeds in a kelp forest provide shelter for juvenile fish and crustaceans. The common sea urchin and blue-rayed limpet can be found grazing on kelps.

Stalked jellyfish **(3)** are unusual animals which live on seaweeds. They have eight arms and are around 2 cm tall. Three UK species are protected by Biodiversity Action Plans.

## TRY SEARCHING FOR

**Under seaweeds:**

1. **Long-legged spider crab** *Macropodia rostrata* (p.110)
2. **Five-bearded rockling** *Ciliata mustela* (p.175)

**On seaweeds:**

3. **Stalked jellyfish** *Haliclystus auricula*
4. **Hydroids or sea firs** (p.84)
5. **Bryozoans or sea mats** (p.150)
6. **Blue-rayed limpet** *Ansates pellucida* (p.126)
7. **Sea slugs** e.g. *Elysia viridis* (p.136)

## 4. Habitats | Rocky shore

# On boulders

**Large areas of boulders and pebbles often have more species associated with them, due to the greater diversity of habitats.**

The sides of boulders are often more sheltered, but all of the surfaces are available for colonization. Boulder shores are rich in life, and the large boulders in particular are worth close examination. Often, a clear zonation pattern is visible on boulders with seaweeds at the top, followed by barnacles, sponges and sea squirts further down.

## TRY SEARCHING FOR

1. **Serrated wrack** *Fucus serratus* (p.192)
2. **Cowrie** *Trivia monacha* (p.125)
3. **Sea lemon** *Archidoris pseudoargus* (p.139)
4. **Baked bean sea squirt** *Dendrodoa grossularia* (p.169)
5. **Painted top shell** *Calliostoma zizyphinum* (p.129)
6. **Star ascidian** *Botryllus schlosseri* (p.170)
7. **Sponges** (e.g. *Dysidia fragilis* p.79)
8. **Honeycomb worm** *Sabellaria alveolata* (p.99)

# Under boulders

**Many creatures live under boulders, attached to the underside either permanently or temporarily. Some animals such as worm pipefish or squat lobsters take shelter in the space below the boulder.**

You could also search the sediment in which the boulder is embedded, as crabs and worms burrow here. However, when searching under boulders, it is important to ensure that you replace them carefully in exactly the same place and also the correct way up. Be careful, do not try to lift heavy boulders!

See the Seashore Code on page 15 for more help.

Searching under a boulder

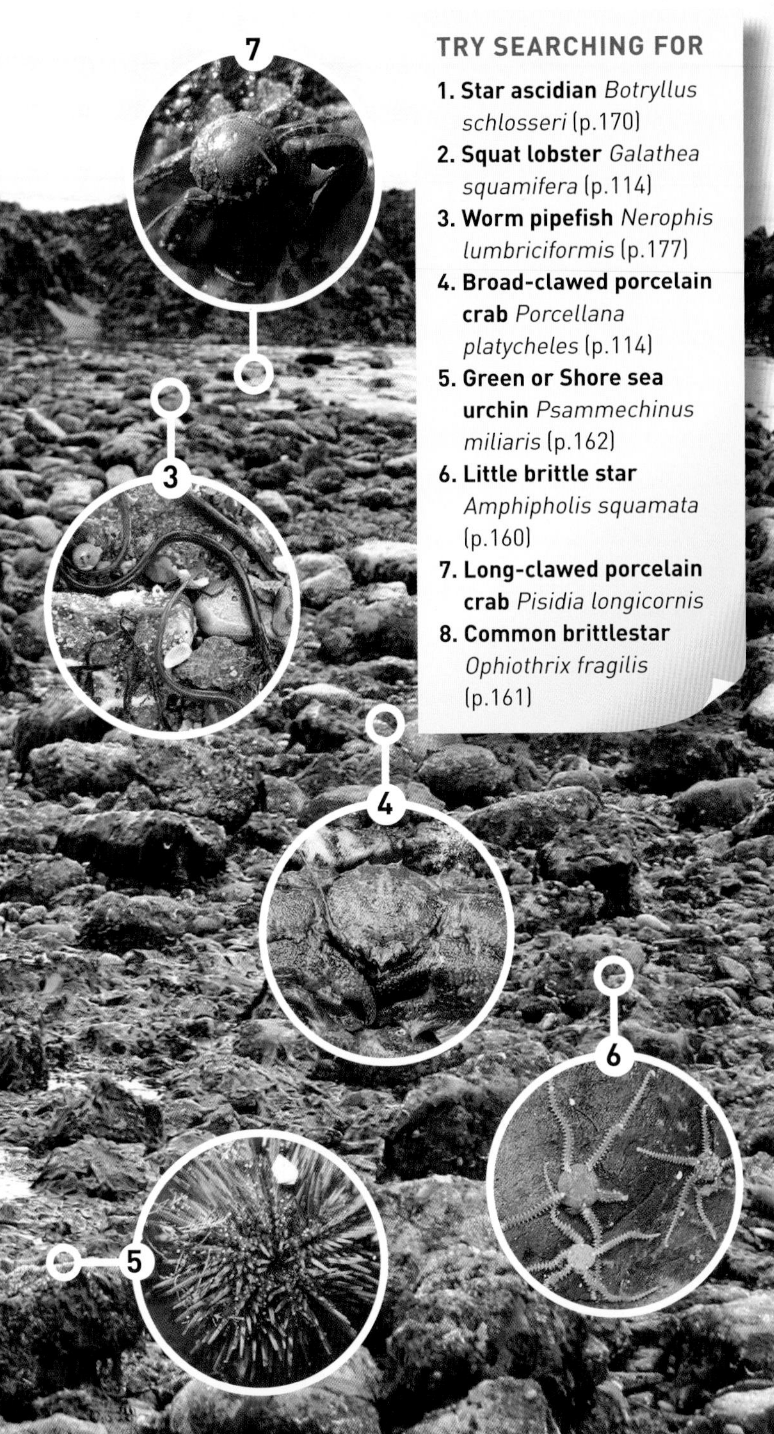


## TRY SEARCHING FOR

1. **Star ascidian** *Botryllus schlosseri* (p.170)
2. **Squat lobster** *Galathea squamifera* (p.114)
3. **Worm pipefish** *Nerophis lumbriciformis* (p.177)
4. **Broad-clawed porcelain crab** *Porcellana platycheles* (p.114)
5. **Green or Shore sea urchin** *Psammechinus miliaris* (p.162)
6. **Little brittle star** *Amphipholis squamata* (p.160)
7. **Long-clawed porcelain crab** *Pisidia longicornis*
8. **Common brittlestar** *Ophiothrix fragilis* (p.161)

## 4. Habitats | Rocky shore

# Strandline

**The strandline is the area on the upper shore where the tide, currents and storms deposit man-made and natural objects from the sea. This can often be seen as a black line of dead seaweed and other vegetation. It defines the high water mark at the top of the beach but the position varies, depending on the level of the tide. Strandlines are found on both rocky and sandy shores (page 22) and each supports its own characteristic wildlife.**

If you look along the strandline, you may find natural debris such as egg-cases of skates and rays, cuttlefish bones, driftwood and empty shells. Unfortunately, you will also find unnatural discarded items such as plastic bottles, drinks cans, sweet wrappers, disposable barbecues, cotton bud sticks, glass, balloons and fishing nets. These can all pose threats to our wildlife and take a long time to disappear or degrade (see page 204). Some items such as plastic fish crates are worth investigating for attached creatures eg. buoy barnacles **(2)**. Insects, birds and mammals all live or feed along the strandline habitat. Sandhoppers **(5)** specialise in eating rotting vegetation and are found in their millions on our beaches. They are an important part of the food web but their populations can be decimated by mechanical beach cleaning **(9)**. A guide to the natural treasures of the strandline can be found on pages 72-75, together with a beach litter quiz on pages 204-205.

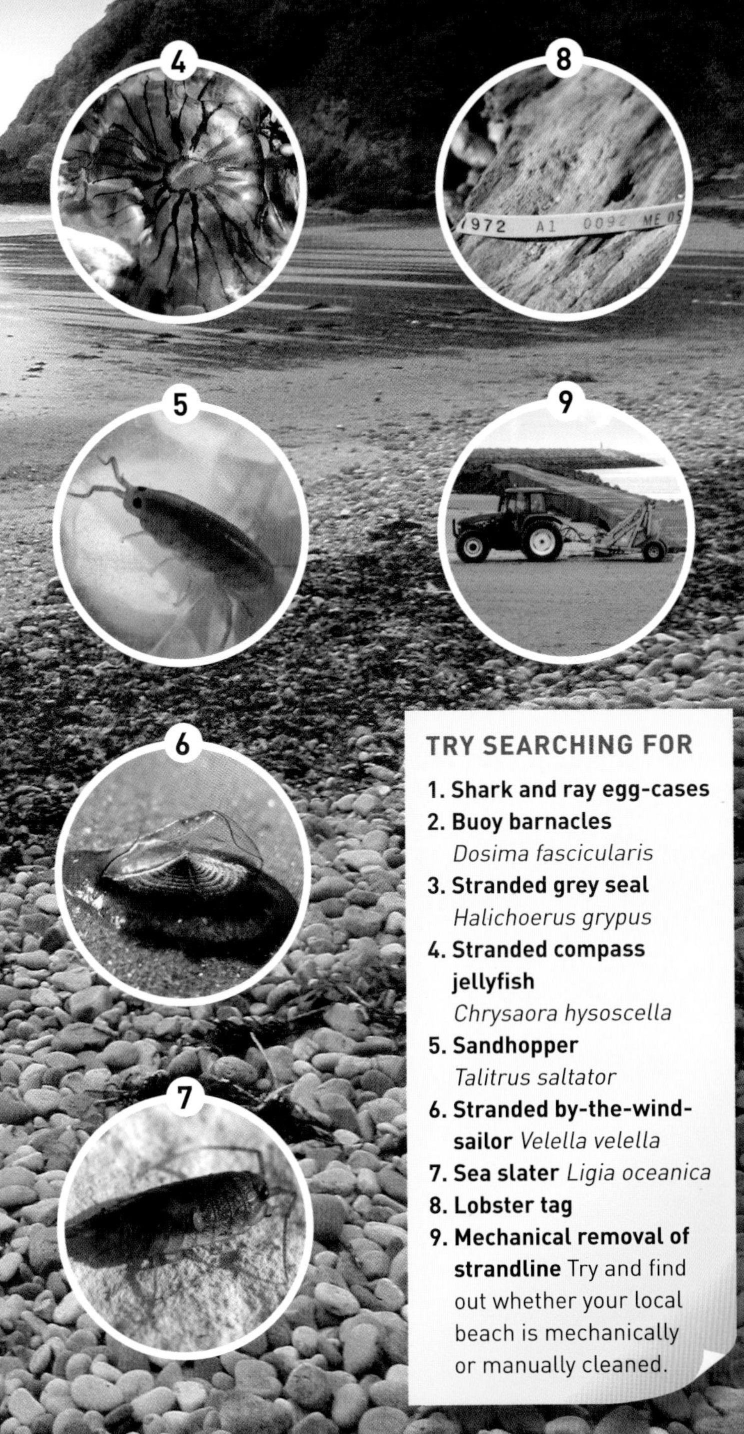


## TRY SEARCHING FOR

1. **Shark and ray egg-cases**
2. **Buoy barnacles** *Dosima fascicularis*
3. **Stranded grey seal** *Halichoerus grypus*
4. **Stranded compass jellyfish** *Chrysaora hysoscella*
5. **Sandhopper** *Talitrus saltator*
6. **Stranded by-the-wind-sailor** *Velella velella*
7. **Sea slater** *Ligia oceanica*
8. **Lobster tag**
9. **Mechanical removal of strandline** Try and find out whether your local beach is mechanically or manually cleaned.

# In and on sand

**Intertidal sand is a difficult place to live. Due to the lack of refuge from predators and the elements, most sandy shore animals live below the surface during all states of the tide.**

Burrowing animals living in the sand are termed the infauna. They can be shallow or deep burrowers. These animals are specially adapted to live in sand and include several species of heart urchin, masked crab, lugworm, sand mason worm and banded wedge shell. They are eaten by birds such as oystercatchers (see below), ringed plovers and purple sandpipers. The tiniest spaces between sand grains, called the **interstitial spaces**, are home to very small animals called the **meiofauna** which includes crustaceans called copepods and worms called nematodes.

Surface-dwelling animals are called the epifauna and are mostly non-residents of the shore, moving in and out with the tide. They include flatfish, lesser sand eel, sand star, brittlestars and necklace shell. They are usually scavengers, feeding on tiny particles sifted from the sand or on **detritus**.

**TRY SEARCHING FOR**

**On the sand:**

1. **Sand star**
   *Astropecten irregularis*
   (p.165)
2. **South-claw hermit crab**
   *Diogenes pugilator*
   (p.119)

Oystercatchers feeding along a sandy shore

## TRY SEARCHING FOR

**In the sand:**

**3. Sand mason worm**
*Lanice conchilega* (p.101)

**4. Sea potato**
*Echinocardium cordatum* (p.165)

**5. Masked crab**
*Corystes cassivelaunus* (p.118)

**6. Pod razor shell**
*Ensis siliqua* (p.147)

**7. Rayed trough shell**
*Mactra stultorum* (p.149)

**8. Purple heart urchin**
*Spatangus purpureus*

## 4. Habitats | Sandy shore

# In pools and on the strandline

Small pools often form on sand in depressions created by wave action. They are worth investigating for species such as lesser sand eel, common hermit crab, brown shrimp and sand goby. If you keep still and wait next to a sandy pool, you may see brown shrimp and juvenile flatfish moving. When disturbed, they quickly bury themselves once again into the sand, hidden behind a cloud of sand grains. A line of rotting seaweed often marks the strandline, where the sea deposits natural and man-made objects.

Many invertebrates shelter amongst this tidal litter. They include sandhoppers, flies, spiders and beetles, some of which are nationally scarce such as the strandline beetle **(4)**. They are vulnerable to human disturbance of their strandline habitat, particularly by removal of driftwood for beach barbecues or decorative purposes. Birds and mammals visit the strandline, and feed on this important food source **(1)** and **(2)**. The best strandlines can often be found on flat sandy beaches backed by sand dunes.

### TRY SEARCHING FOR

**On the strandline:**

1. **Evidence of birds feeding along the strandline**
   e.g. heron footprint
2. **Evidence of mammal feeding along the strandline**
   e.g. fox footprint
3. **Sandhoppers feeding on rotting seaweed**
4. **Strandline beetle**
   *Eurynebria complanata*

## TRY SEARCHING FOR

**In pools:**

**4. Brown shrimp**
*Crangon crangon* (p.117)

**5. Sand goby**
*Pomatoschistus minutus* (p.179)

**6. Flatfish e.g. Dover sole**
*Solea solea* (p.179)

**7. Common hermit crab**
*Pagurus bernhardus* (p.113)

**8. Little cuttlefish**
*Sepiola atlantica*

**9. Plaice (juvenile)**
*Pleuronectes platessa*

4

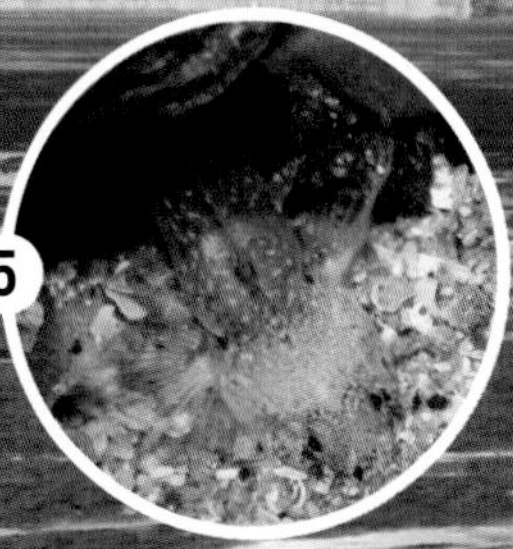

5

6

7

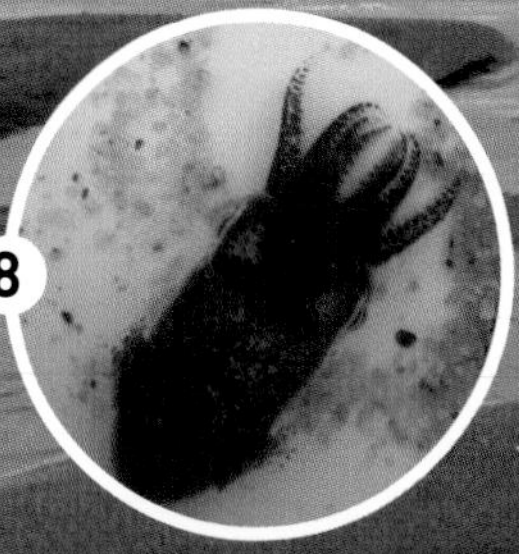

8

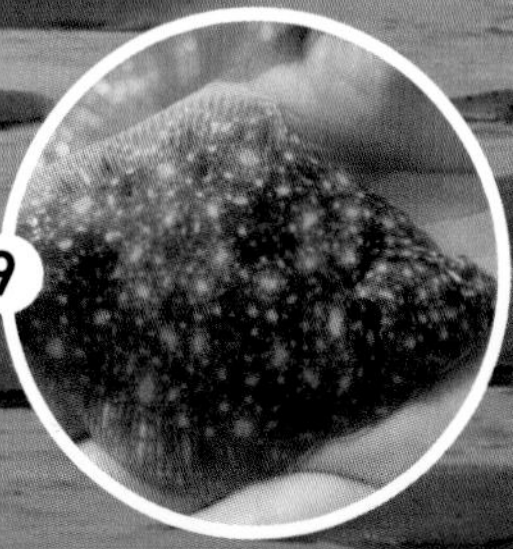

9

## 4. Habitats | Sandy shore

# Signs of life

**At first glance, vast expanses of sandy beach may seem to have no visible life. If you look closely, however, you will see the signs of many animals that live there.**

There may be worm casts on the surface, siphons protruding from the sand, or slight craters. These tell-tale signs give an indication of what may live burrowed or buried below.

If you dig in the sand below these signs very carefully, you may discover what creature these signs belong to. Alternatively, try sieving the sand with a fine-meshed garden or kitchen sieve and you will be amazed at what lies hidden.

**QUIZ: SIGNS OF LIFE**

The images on these pages show some typical surface signs or evidence of animal life. See if you can guess what creatures may be hiding in the sand. This will also help you to match the trails and casts you find on your safari with their rightful owners. The answers on pages 66-67 may surprise you!

5
6
7
8
9
10
11

# Signs of life answers

How many correct answers did you have? Use your new knowledge on your next sandy shore safari to locate the creatures hidden beneath your feet.

1 A Mollusc *Abra alba*

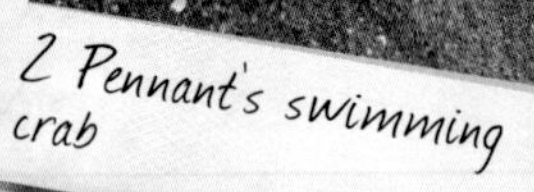
2 Pennant's swimming crab

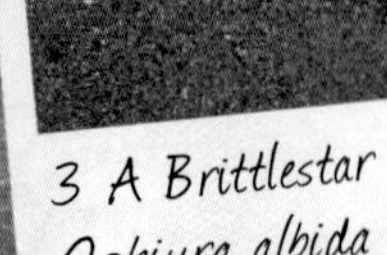
3 A Brittlestar *Ophiura albida*

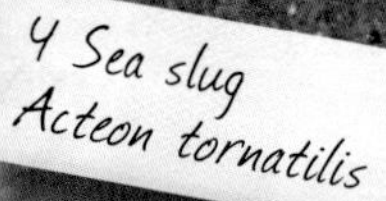
4 Sea slug *Acteon tornatilis*

5 Banded wedge shell

6 Sea potato

7 Rayed trough shell

8 Striped venus clam

9 Masked crab

10 Necklace shell

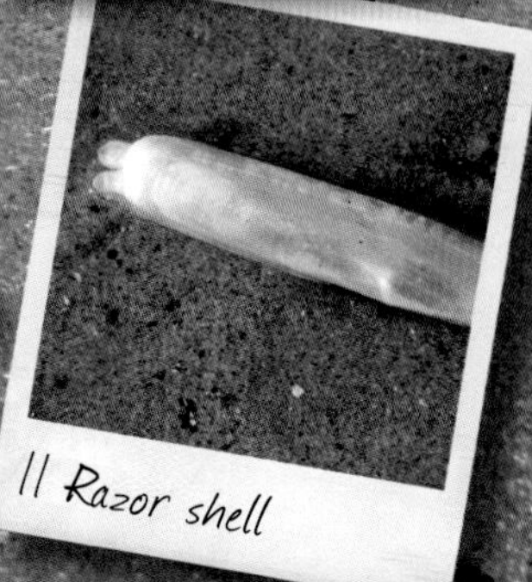
11 Razor shell

# 5. Beachcombing

**Beachcombing is a great way to introduce children to natural history. By walking along any beach (both rocky and sandy), following the line of dead seaweed at the top of the shore on the strandline, you will find many items deposited by the tides and currents. This is often termed flotsam and jetsam.**

Amongst many man-made items such as discarded fishing line and plastic litter, you can find an assortment of beautiful natural items including shells and mermaid's purses. Further down the shore, you may also find stranded animals such as jellyfish. Test yourself by arranging your finds into 'trash' or 'treasure'.

Collecting shells from the beach is great fun, but make sure that they are empty before you take them home. Each sandy beach will have a different mollusc community, and this can be sampled by searching the strandline and shore for empty shells. When you have identified your shells, you can build up a picture of what lives on your beach, or what might have been deposited there from offshore.

Use the shell guide on pages 72-73 and the strandline guide on page 74-75 to help you to identify your strandline treasures.


**Stranded creatures** 70

**Strandline treasures – shell guide** 72

**Assorted strandline treasures** 74

## PROJECT:

### STRANDLINE SCAVENGER HUNT

You can play this game in a family or school group. Split into teams and head for the strandline with your list of what to collect. Only collect items which you can return safely and without damaging the environment. Do not collect anything dangerous or unhygienic. Check that all shells are empty.

Try to collect the following items:

- at least 1000 grains of sand
- something slimy
- something delicate
- something green
- a spiral
- a piece of driftwood
- something smooth
- a feather
- a cuttlefish bone
- 20 pebbles
- something spiky
- something unnatural
- some rope
- something red

Now that you have collected lots of interesting items, use them to make a beach sculpture of your favourite seashore animal. You can also collect anything else you might need from the strandline. Use your imagination and come up with your own team design. Take a photo of your completed sculpture before the sea reclaims it!

## PROJECT:

### TRASH OR TREASURE

Search the strandline and investigate the natural and unnatural items you find. Arrange them into groups depending on whether they are 'trash' (man-made rubbish), or 'treasure' (natural items). Look at the natural items, and see if you can identify them and the creatures to which they belong, such as egg-cases, mollusc shells, crabs shells and bones. The strandline guide on pages 72-75 will help you. The 'treasure' you find will give you a clue as to what lives on the beach and also offshore. With care, look closely at the 'trash' or beach litter and see if you can guess its source and composition.

There may be clues on the packaging. See if you can guess how long your litter takes to degrade and try the quiz on pages 204-205.

# Stranded creatures

**After storms or gales, it is worth looking along the strandline for unusual objects that have been washed up. Some of my most interesting finds have included stranded jellyfish, sea gooseberries and goose barnacles.**

Often in bad weather, creatures are pushed or blown off-course out at sea, and become disorientated, leading them to strand on our beaches. Keep an eye out for loggerhead turtles, Portuguese man-of-war, and marine mammals such as dolphins, seals, porpoises and whales. Information on where to report live or dead strandings is given on page 213. Marine litter and debris, such as plastic fish trays, are also worth investigating for attached creatures such as species of goose barnacle.

## Stranded mammals

Dolphins, porpoises and whales are marine mammals which live around our coasts. They sometimes wash ashore dead but occasionally they may be alive. There are many reasons why these animals are found stranded on the shore. These include disease, trauma, malnutrition and becoming lost. It is very important to report a stranding and details of how to do this (depending on whether the animal is dead or alive) are given on page 213. You should avoid touching stranded animals as they can carry diseases.

## Sea gooseberry

*Pleurobrachia pileus*

Also called a comb jelly, the sea gooseberry seems to shimmer as it swims along, as light is reflected by rows of tiny hairs on the body. It is transparent and has two long tentacles, but these may be contracted and not visible. Mass strandings of these animals often occur in the summer. The animals are up to 2 cm long.

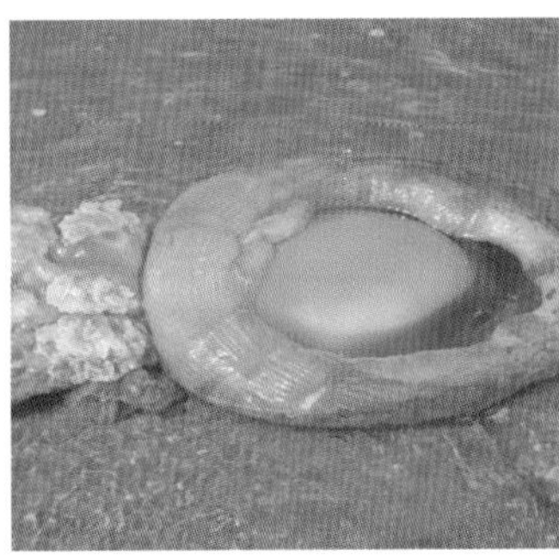

## Dustbin lid or barrel jellyfish

*Rhizostoma octopus*

This large jellyfish is confined to southern and western coastal waters of the British Isles. It can be found stranded on the shore or in rockpools. The colour varies from white to yellow or shades of blue and pink. It has 4 pairs of large mouth arms underneath but no tentacles. The thick, dome shaped bell can be up to 90 cm in diameter. In summer and autumn, it may occur in swarms. The barrel jellyfish has no sting but may cause a rash. Report your jellyfish sightings (of any species) to the organisations on page 212.

## Common Goose barnacle

*Lepas anatifera*

The common goose barnacle is often found stranded in large groups, attached to flotsam such as plastic crates or buoys, pieces of wood, rope or polystyrene. It has a long flexible stalk called a **peduncle** and a white shell composed of five smooth plates with a dark brown skin. Goose barnacles are often found washed up on the shore on western coasts of Britain and Ireland, especially after westerly gales. The stalk can be 4 – 90 cm long and the shell up to 5 cm long. This large group stranded on Oxwich Beach, Gower, is attached to a large log.

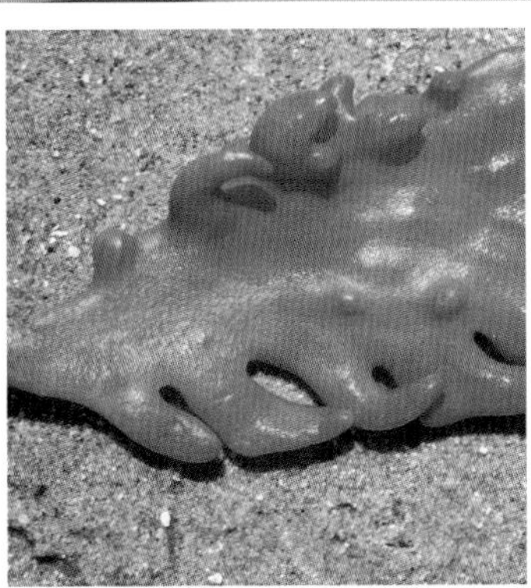

## Sea chervil

*Alcyonidium diaphanum*

Sea chervil is a type of colonial animal called a bryozoan which is widespread around Britain and Ireland. It can be smooth or knobbly with a gelatinous texture and is usually attached to rocks on the lower shore and in the sub-littoral zone. It is responsible for a skin allergy called 'Dogger Bank Itch' sometimes experienced by fishermen.

# Strandline treasures – shell guide

Common wentletrap

Mussel

Keyhole limpet

Banded venus

Flat periwinkle

Necklace shell

Rayed trough shell

Saddle oyster

Painted top shell

Grey top shell

Common or Edible periwinkle

Banded carpet shell

Common whelk

Common limpet

Pod razor shell

Razor shell

Great scallop
Dog whelk
Pullet carpet shell
Alder's necklace shell
Cockle
Blue-rayed limpet
Common oyster
Striped venus clam
Spotted cowrie
*Acteon tornatilis*
Flat top shell
Common piddock
Turret shell
Spiny cockle
Netted Dog whelk
Common otter shell
Variegated scallop

# Assorted strandline treasures

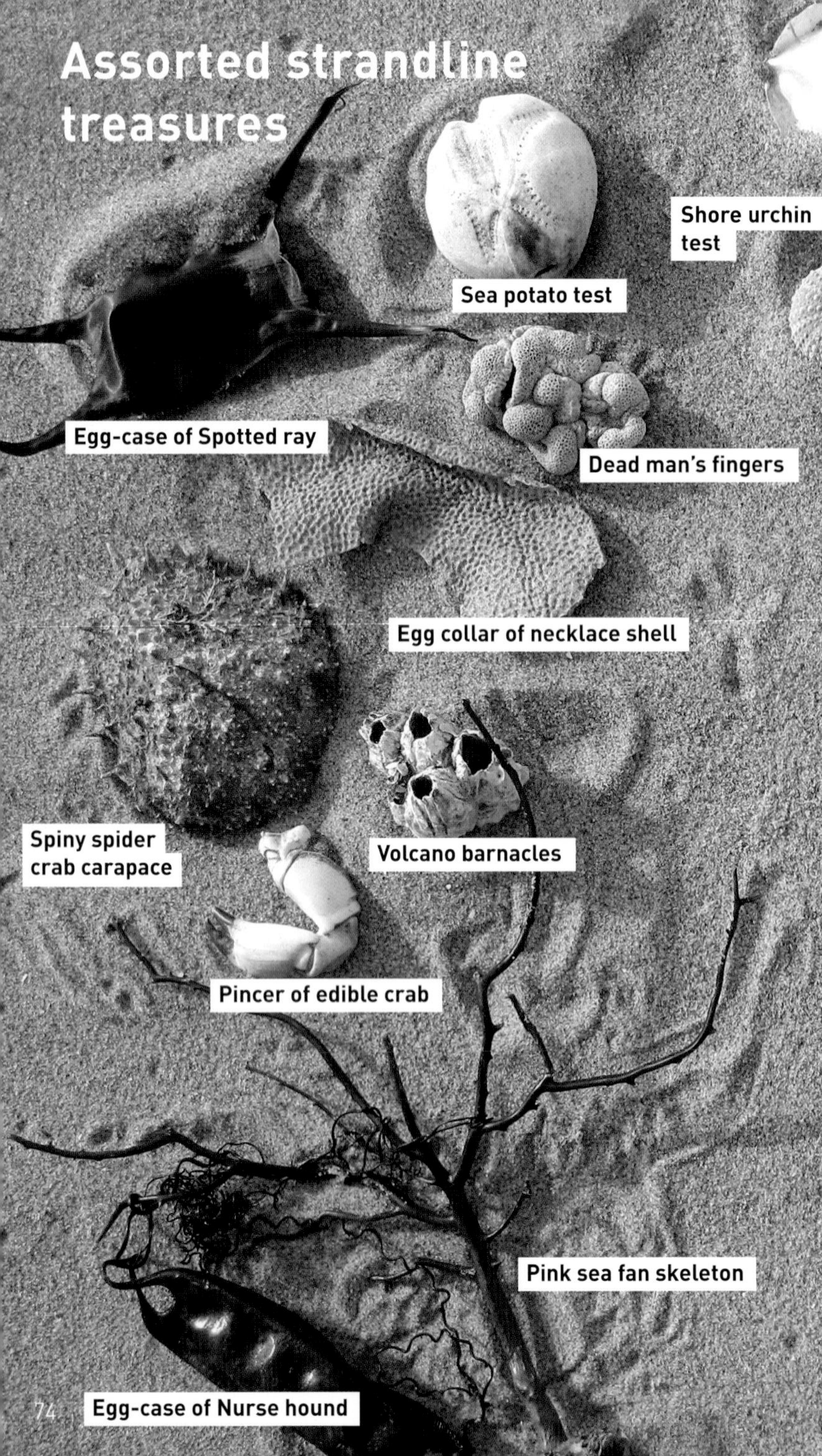

Mermaid's fingers sponge

Seashore Safaris

# 6. Animal life

**The animal life of rocky and sandy shores is abundant and diverse, and examples can be found from all the major groups or phyla of the animal kingdom. However, the types of animals inhabiting rocky shores differ from those on sandy shores.**

On rocky shores, the many micro-habitats (see Chapter 4) present provide homes and shelter for a wide range of species, but the abundance and distribution of animal species depends on the amount of wave action. Inhabitants of a rocky shore include many **invertebrates**, from the simplest porifera or sponges to molluscs like sea slugs, and the more advanced vertebrates, including bony fish.

The number of species and variety of animals on a sandy shore is much less than that found on a rocky shore. Exposure to wave action is also the single most important factor determining the variety and abundance of life on a sandy shore. Most species live near low water level. The types of animals living in a sandy habitat must be able to dig, burrow or tunnel into the sediment to escape any hazardous conditions. This limits the number of species found. Bristle worms (polychaetes) and bivalve molluscs dominate life here. All rocky and sandy shore animals are adapted to feed and breed during the short time in which they are covered by the tide.

In this section, a wide range of the more common intertidal animal species is included, along with information on where to locate them, and their key features. They are arranged in **taxonomic order** from sponges to fish. Both common and scientific names of species have been used. Common names, however, will vary across the country. Many species have never been given common names. All scientific names stated are in accordance with the World Register of Marine Species (WoRMS).

The types of animals found will also vary from the north to the south of the country. Where 'widespread' is stated as a distribution, this refers to the fact that the species can be found all around the coasts of Britain and Ireland. A guide to the most common types of eggs you are likely to find on a seashore safari is included. This will help you to identify which creature laid them. Please remember to follow the Seashore Code on page 15 each time you search for or handle any animal on the shore. When you have identified your finds, you can record this information in your field notebook (see page 17).

**Porifera or sponges** 78
**Cnidaria** (Hydroids or sea firs, corals and sea anemones) 82
**Worms** 94
**Crustaceans** (Barnacles, crabs, lobsters, prawns, shrimps, and sandy shore crabs) 104
**Molluscs** (Chitons, sea snails, sea slugs and bivalves) 120
**Bryozoans or sea mats** 150
**Echinoderms** (Sea cucumbers, crinoids, starfish, brittlestars, sea urchins and sandy shore echinoderms) 152
**Tunicates and vertebrates** (Sea squirts and fish) 166
**Who laid these eggs?** 180

**NOTE:**

Some species are very difficult to identify, may vary greatly in colour and size and the key features may not be obvious. In some cases, it is easy to confuse one species with another. For example, the Five-bearded and Shore rockling both occur on rocky shores. By recording useful information about your finds (p.17), and by taking photographs or by making sketches, it will be easier to research the type of animal you have located.

# Porifera or sponges

**Porifera or sponges are amongst the simplest types of multi-celled animals, and cannot move about.**

The body of a sponge consists of two layers with a space between, filled with seawater. Sponges filter feed by sieving a continuous current of water and extracting tiny food particles. The excess water is expelled through large volcano-shaped openings on the surface called **oscula**. Sponges are often very colourful, and their size and shape varies with the conditions in which they live.

Their basic framework is strengthened with tiny pointed spikes called **spicules**. These are made of lime or silica. Many sponges are difficult to identify in the field, and identification often relies on the shape of these spicules, requiring magnification under a microscope. Sponges are found only on rocky shores as they need a firm surface to live on. They can occur alone (solitary) or in groups (colonies). About 30 different species of sponge can be found regularly between the tides.

## CREATURE FEATURES

- Simplest of animals with many cells
- Colonial or solitary
- Cannot move about
- Filter feeding animals
- Most intertidal species form sheets or low mounds
- External surface has small inhalant pores or **ostia** and one or more large exhalant holes called **oscula**
- Can be very colourful
- Size and shape is very variable
- Most species are difficult to identify

## A sponge

*Hymeniacidon perleve*

**Size:** up to 20 cm or more across
**Colour:** usually blood-red
**Zone:** mid to lower shore
**Habitat:** on rock or on seaweeds and in crevices
**Distribution:** widespread
More abundant on the south, south west and west coasts of Britain
**Field notes:** This species of sponge forms small sheets or mounds usually with a rough, lumpy surface although it can be smooth. It prefers slightly silty environments and smells sweet.

## A sponge

*Dysidia fragilis*

**Size:** usually less than 15 cm across
**Colour:** whitish or grey
**Zone:** lower shore
**Habitat:** under and on boulders, overhangs
**Distribution:** widespread
**Field notes:** The surface of this sponge looks spiky because of spongin fibres lifting the surface layer.

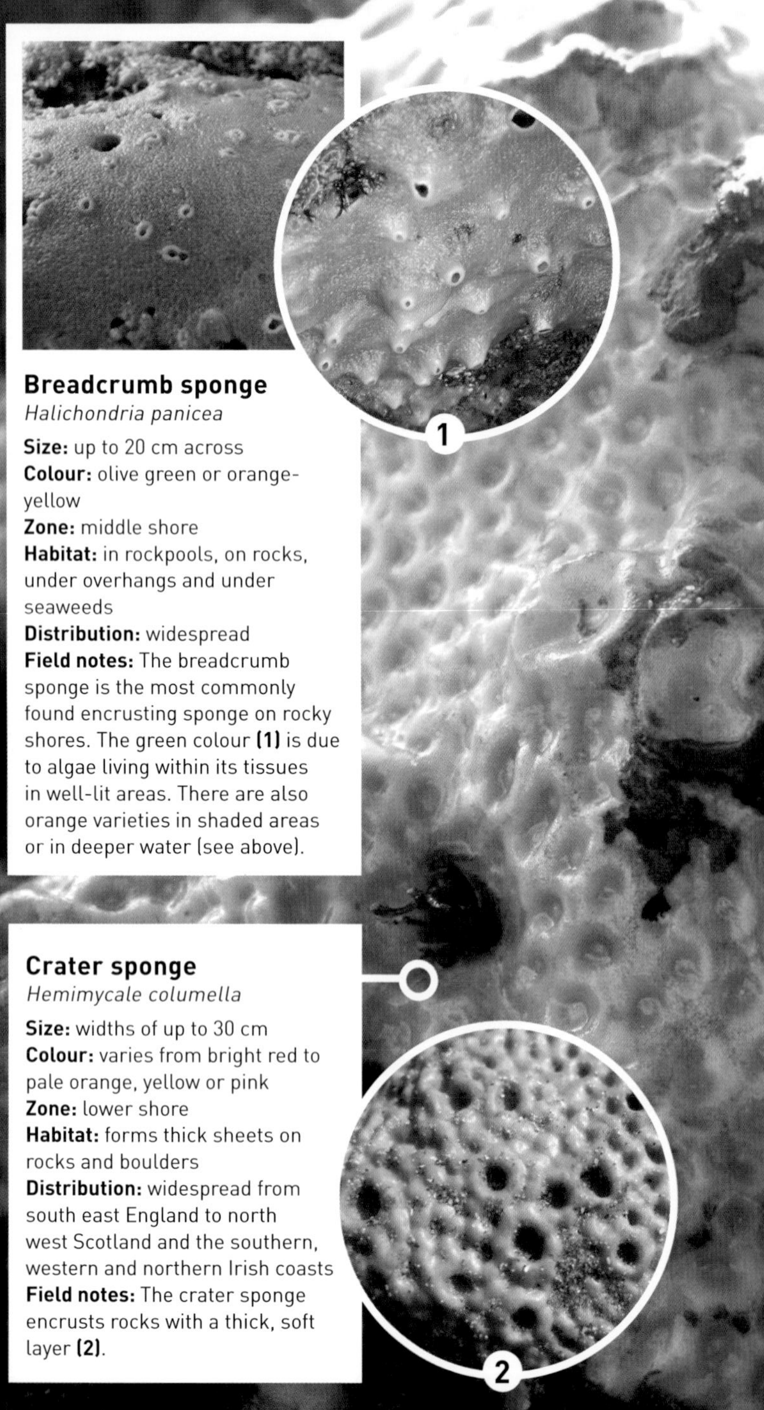


## Breadcrumb sponge

*Halichondria panicea*

**Size:** up to 20 cm across
**Colour:** olive green or orange-yellow
**Zone:** middle shore
**Habitat:** in rockpools, on rocks, under overhangs and under seaweeds
**Distribution:** widespread
**Field notes:** The breadcrumb sponge is the most commonly found encrusting sponge on rocky shores. The green colour **(1)** is due to algae living within its tissues in well-lit areas. There are also orange varieties in shaded areas or in deeper water (see above).

## Crater sponge

*Hemimycale columella*

**Size:** widths of up to 30 cm
**Colour:** varies from bright red to pale orange, yellow or pink
**Zone:** lower shore
**Habitat:** forms thick sheets on rocks and boulders
**Distribution:** widespread from south east England to north west Scotland and the southern, western and northern Irish coasts
**Field notes:** The crater sponge encrusts rocks with a thick, soft layer **(2)**.

## Purse sponge

*Grantia compressa*

**Size:** 1 – 2 cm high, 0.5 – 1 cm across
**Colour:** white or cream
**Zone:** lower shore
**Habitat:** on rock or on seaweeds and in crevices
**Distribution:** widespread
**Field notes:** The purse sponge is a tapering sac-shaped sponge with a single osculum. It is attached at its base by a short stalk to rock or seaweed, and is often found in small groups. The purse sponge is an annual species which dies in the spring, after releasing larvae into the water.

## Pencil sponge

*Ciocalypta penicillus*

**Size:** base 10 – 20 cm diameter, conical growths 5 – 10 cm high
**Colour:** various – usually white to yellow
**Zone:** lower shore
**Habitat:** attached to rock surfaces often covered in sand or gravel
**Distribution:** west and south coasts of Britain and around the coast of Ireland
**Field notes:** This sponge consists of a cushion-shaped base attached to rocks with pointed, conical growths protruding from this. Only the pointed growths are usually visible.

## Golf ball sponge

*Tethya aurantium*

**Size:** up to 6 cm diameter
**Colour:** orange or yellow
**Zone:** lower shore
**Habitat:** under overhangs and attached to rock
**Distribution:** south west England, the west coast of Wales, western Scotland and most Irish coasts
**Field notes:** The golf ball sponge is shaped like a small orange, and covered in warts or tubercles, often with a layer of silt.

# Cnidaria

**Anemones, corals, jellyfish and hydroids (sea firs) all belong to the phylum Cnidaria.**

These animals are soft bodied polyps with a 'flower-like' shape. All Cnidarians are characterized by the presence of stinging cells called **cnidae** or **nematocysts**, especially on the tentacles. Nematocysts consist of a capsule with a coiled thread inside, armed with stinging cells. These are fired into the prey to stun or paralyse it, and are also used as a defence mechanism. The number of tentacles can vary from fewer than ten to several hundred.

**Hydroids or sea firs** 84
**Corals** 86
**Sea anemones** 88

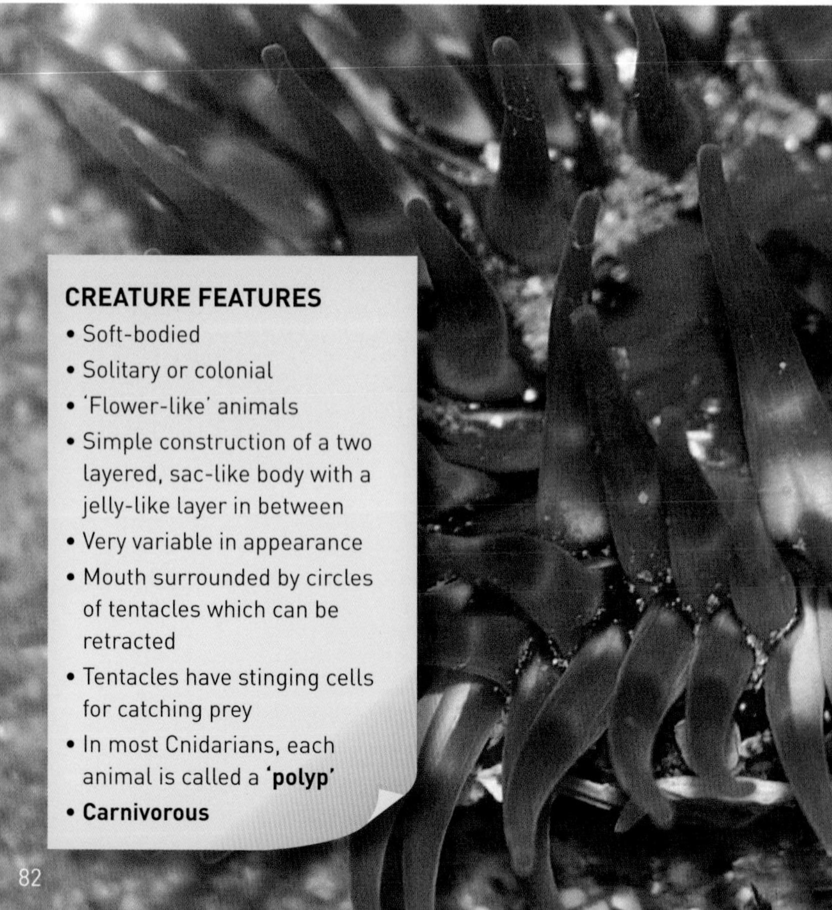

## CREATURE FEATURES

- Soft-bodied
- Solitary or colonial
- 'Flower-like' animals
- Simple construction of a two layered, sac-like body with a jelly-like layer in between
- Very variable in appearance
- Mouth surrounded by circles of tentacles which can be retracted
- Tentacles have stinging cells for catching prey
- In most Cnidarians, each animal is called a **'polyp'**
- **Carnivorous**

## Dahlia anemone

*Urticina felina*

**Size:** up to 20 cm across tentacles
**Colour:** variable, banded or plain
**Zone:** lower shore
**Habitat:** in rockpools, crevices or surge gullies
**Distribution:** widespread
**Field notes:** The dahlia anemone is one of the largest British sea anemones, and attaches to rocks by a thick, muscular base. The column is covered in 'warts' and often stone and shell fragments stick to these. The dahlia anemone looks very different out of water as it pulls in its tentacles to protect itself at low tide **(1)**.The two images of the anemone in water show red and purple varieties.

1

## 6. Animal life | Cnidaria

# Hydroids or sea firs

**Hydroids or sea firs belong to the class Hydrozoa. They are the simplest Cnidarians and are usually formed by colonial polyps.**

A colony is formed from many upright shoots, joined at the base. Individual polyps may have different jobs within the colony such as feeding, defence or reproduction. The main stem can be branched so that they appear bushy or feathery. The colony grows in size by the addition of new branches and polyps.

The feeding polyp is like a little 'cup' from which the animal extends its tentacles to feed. Only a few species are characteristic of the rocky shore. They are difficult to identify.

**CREATURE FEATURES**

- Colonial animals
- Difficult to identify with the naked eye, so only a few examples of the more common and easily identified species are included
- Polyps often grow close together
- Look like tiny fir trees or ferns
- Occur mostly in rockpools or on seaweeds

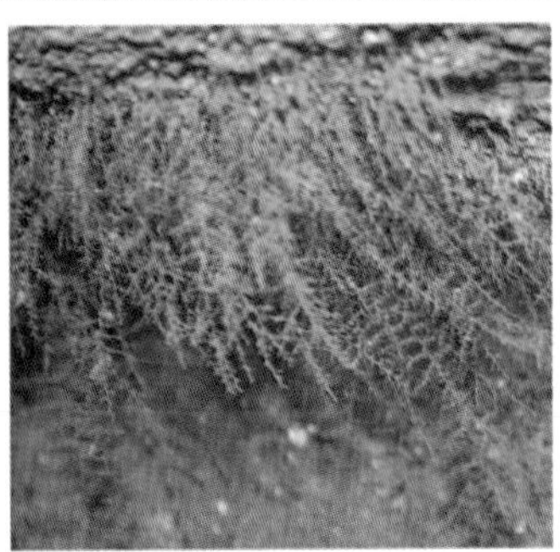

## A hydroid

*Obelia longissima*

**Size:** up to 20 cm long
**Colour:** pale white to brownish
**Zone:** lower shore
**Habitat:** on algae and on sheltered rocks in rockpools
**Distribution:** widespread
**Field notes:** This hydroid has a long stem and shorter side branches. It is a passive carnivore and feeds on prey swimming into it, which is killed or stunned by stinging cells on its tentacles. Its prey includes tiny zooplankton and larvae of other animals. The animal lives in a bell-shaped cup. The hydroid itself is an important food source for animals such as nudibranchs and polychaete worms.

## A hydroid

*Dynamena pumila*

**Size:** stems up to 3 cm high
**Colour:** pale grey brown or fawnish
**Zone:** middle shore downwards
**Habitat:** commonly attached to serrated wrack (*Fucus serratus*), bladder wrack (*Fucus vesiculosus*) and kelp species and on rock
**Distribution:** widespread on moderately exposed to sheltered rocky shores
**Field notes:** This is one of the most common hydroids on the shore. It forms upright, usually unbranched stems with a 'zigzag' appearance. The polyps live in pairs of tiny cups attached to the stems. This hydroid is most abundant on shores subject to strong water movement from tidal streams or wave action.

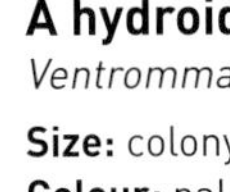

## A hydroid

*Ventromma halecioides*

**Size:** colony up to 5 cm
**Colour:** pale white
**Zone:** lower shore
**Habitat:** on other hydroids, algae and rocks in rockpools
**Distribution:** scattered locations around British Isles
**Field notes:** This hydroid has a delicate feathery appearance.

**Scarlet and gold star coral**
*Balanophyllia regia*

**Size:** 1 cm diameter
**Colour:** bright yellow-orange
**Zone:** lower shore
**Habitat:** attached to rocks in surge gulleys or under overhangs
**Distribution:** south west England, the Scilly Isles and south west Pembrokeshire
**Field notes:** This brightly coloured cup coral has up to 48 tentacles arranged in groups of six around the mouth. It has a hard external skeleton made of calcium carbonate.

## 6. Animal life | Cnidaria

# Corals

**It is amazing to think that we do indeed have colourful corals existing on our shores, and they are not just restricted to tropical or sub-tropical waters.**

Intertidal corals may be hard or soft and colonial or solitary. They are characterized by feeding polyps and tentacles. The soft corals such as dead man's fingers belong to the Order **Alcyonacea** and the stony corals such as Devonshire cup coral to the Order **Scleractinia**. Soft corals are composed of a soft, spongy colony strengthened by spicules. The polyps have eight tentacles arranged in a circle. There are only three species in Britain and Ireland.

Stony corals have a hard **exoskeleton** called the **corallum** which is made of limestone. The polyps have at least 12 tentacles, arranged in two circles. Only solitary stony corals are found on the rocky shores of Britain and Ireland.

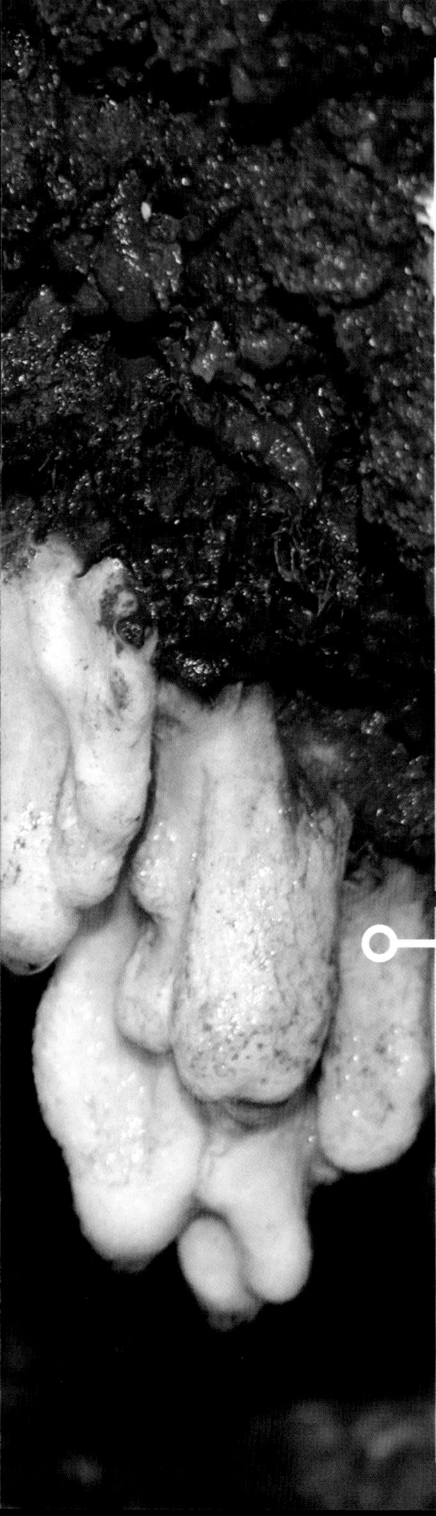

## Devonshire cup coral

*Caryophyllia smithii*

**Size:** up to 3 cm diameter
**Colour:** variable but usually brightly coloured white, pink, orange, green
**Zone:** extreme lower shore
**Habitat:** on rocks, shaded crevices and overhangs and deep pools
**Distribution:** all around the south and west coasts of Britain and Ireland
**Field notes:** A solitary hard, stony coral, it has up to 80 tentacles with small knobs on the ends. There is often a distinct 'zigzag' pattern around the mouth.

## Dead man's fingers

*Alcyonium digitatum*

**Size:** each finger up to 20 cm
**Colour:** white, pinkish or yellowish
**Zone:** lower shore
**Habitat:** under overhangs, attached to rocks
**Distribution:** widespread
**Field notes**: Each finger is a colony of soft coral, made up of tiny animals called polyps. When the tide is in, the polyp extends its eight feeding tentacles, often in areas of strong water movement. The colonies in the photograph are out of water. Individual polyps are held together by a jelly-like mass strengthened by calcareous spicules. They can live for over 25 years.

# Sea anemones

**Sea anemones belong to the Class Anthozoa and the Order Actinaria. They are armed with large numbers of stinging cells called cnidae, which they use to paralyse or stun their prey.**

They are primitive creatures, with a mouth surrounded by a ring of tentacles, leading to a simple stomach. The body is soft and jelly-like, and it is often brightly coloured. Water pressure inside the body maintains the anemone's shape. On a rocky shore it is usually attached to rocks by the base, or burrowed in sand or shingle at the base of rockpools or surge gulleys. A few species of sea anemone are adapted to living burrowed in soft sand or mud. They can be seen on the lower shore if you look carefully in shallow pools or on the surface. However, they are usually quite small and well-camouflaged against wet sand, so may be difficult to spot. Sea anemones can use their bases as a sort of foot to move about. At low tide, most anemones can retract or pull the tentacles into the body for protection.

When identifying sea anemones, it is best not to rely solely on their colour as a feature, as this can be extremely variable.

## CREATURE FEATURES

- Solitary
- Attached with a sucker-like basal disc on rocks or burrowed into soft sediment
- Between the base and the tentacles is the cylinder-shaped **column**
- Simple unbranched tentacles arranged in circular multiples of 6
- Tentacles are armed with stinging cells
- Mostly carnivorous
- Many are very colourful
- Shape and size very variable
- Highly specialised polyps
- Around 12 species commonly found on our rocky shores

## Strawberry anemone

*Actinia fragacea*

**Size:** up to 10 cm high and up to 10 cm across tentacles
**Colour:** red with green/yellow spots/flecks like pips on a strawberry
**Zone:** lower shore
**Habitat:** on rocks and in rockpools usually in shaded places
**Distribution:** mainly south and west coasts of Britain and Ireland
**Field notes:** Similar to the beadlet anemone, the strawberry anemone is larger and much less common. The image below **(1)** shows how different the strawberry anemone looks when out of water, with its tentacles retracted.

1

## Gem anemone

*Aulactinia verrucosa*

**Size:** up to 6 cm across
**Colour:** varied, tentacles banded green, grey or pink
**Zone:** lower shore
**Habitat:** in crevices, surge gullies and rockpools
**Distribution:** classed as a southern species reaching its northern limit in the British Isles. Most common on south and west shores of Britain, and present on all Irish coasts. Recorded at a few locations in south west.
**Field Notes:** The gem anemone has about 48 tentacles which are striped and arranged in circles of six. When closed **(2)**, it resembles a small sea urchin **test** (page 74). The column has six rows of small white warts or **verrucae**.

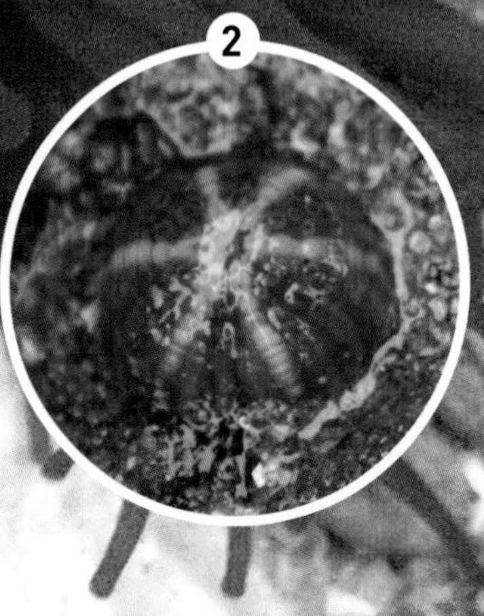

2

## Snakelocks anemone

*Anemonia viridis*

**Size:** up to 5 cm diameter
**Colour:** column brownish, tentacles brown, grey or bright green with purple tips
**Zone:** lower shore
**Habitat:** in rockpools and on rocks
**Distribution:** south and west coasts of Britain and Ireland and north to Scotland
**Field notes:** In well-lit areas, tiny algae called **zooxanthellae** live in the tentacles of the snakelocks anemone, giving it the green colour (see background image). In shaded areas, it is a dull khaki grey colour (see image above). This anemone has up to 200 tentacles, which rarely fully contract and, out of water, it hangs down limply. You may be lucky to spot a Leach's spider crab *Inachus phalangium* (p.112) living in the centre of large snakelocks anemones **(1)**. Be careful when investigating as these anemones can sting you!

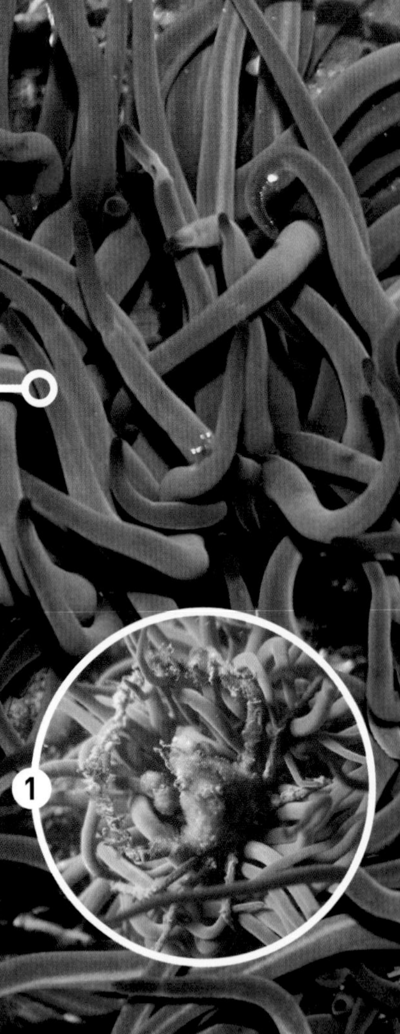


### DID YOU KNOW?

The grey sea slug (p138) can feed on the snakelocks anemone as it is immune to poison from the stinging cells. It stores these and uses them as its own form of defence against predators.

## Elegant anemone

*Sagartia elegans*

**Size:** up to 4 cm diameter
**Colour:** very variable with five main colour varieties. The variety shown (*venusta*) is bright orange with white tentacles and white spots on the column
**Zone:** lower middle shore downwards
**Habitat:** in rockpools, attached to rocks, under overhangs and in crevices
**Distribution:** widespread
**Field notes:** The elegant anemone has up to 200 tentacles and is often found in large groups. When disturbed, they can withdraw into crevices or holes.

## Beadlet anemone

*Actinia equina*

**Size:** up to 5 cm high and 7 cm across tentacles
**Colour:** red, green, brown or orange
**Zone:** upper to lower shore
**Habitat:** on rocks and in rockpools
**Distribution:** widespread
**Field notes:** One of most common anemones found on the shore, the beadlet anemone can live for more than three years. At low tide, this anemone looks like a 'blob' of red jelly stuck to the rocks as it retracts its tentacles to help retain moisture. In water, it has six circles of around 192 tentacles around the mouth and looks like a flower. There are prominent bright blue 'beads' called acrorhagi below the tentacles where the stinging cells are stored. The image below **(2)** shows a green variety of beadlet anemone out of water.

# Sandy shore Sea anemones

## A sea anemone

*Sagartiogeton undatus*

**Size:** column up to 12 cm high, 6 cm across base
**Colour:** column pale yellow and striped. Tentacles almost transparent with white line
**Zone:** lower shore
**Habitat:** buried in sand or mud, especially on sheltered shores
**Distribution:** south and west coasts of Britain and Ireland
**Field notes:** This anemone has up to 200 long tentacles, arranged in groups of six. The base of the anemone is attached to a stone or shell beneath the surface of the sand.

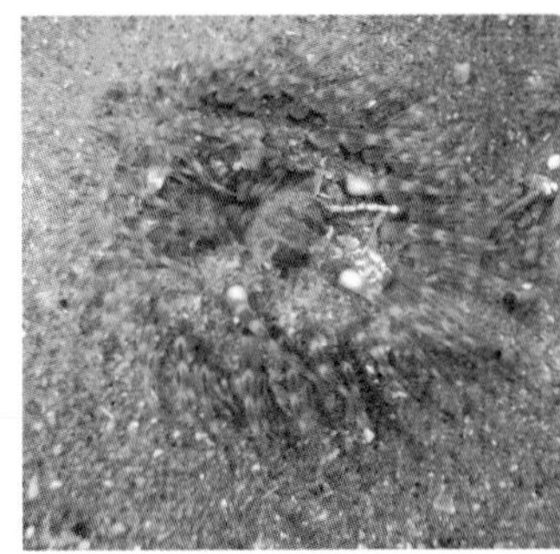

## Daisy anemone

*Cereus pedunculatus*

**Size:** up to 10 cm across, column height up to 12 cm
**Colour:** varied, usually blue-grey, tentacles banded and mottled
**Zone:** middle to lower shore
**Habitat:** in holes and crevices, buried in sand or mud in rockpools and on sandy shores.
**Distribution:** south and west coasts of Britain and north to Scotland, and all around the Irish coast
**Field notes:** There are 500-700 short tentacles arranged in multiples of six. The column is dark coloured and trumpet shaped, often with sand and shingle fragments attached. The insert **(1)** shows a Daisy anemone on a rocky shore, living amongst a bed of common mussels.

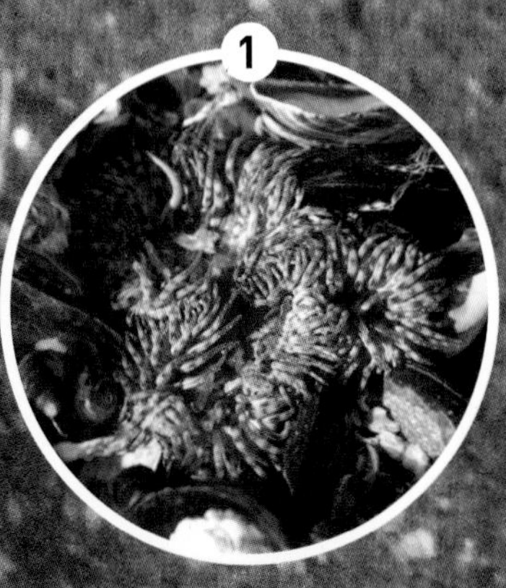

1

6. Animal life

# Worms

**The Phylum Annelida or true worms have a long rounded body made up of many segments. The most common marine group is the Class Polychaeta or bristle worms which are either active, free-moving burrowers, or are living in a tube.**

Bundles of bristles (chaetae) are found on the sides of the worms. Many species of **Polychaete** can be found on our shores, though most are small and easily overlooked. Most of the tube-dwelling worms themselves will not be seen at low tide as they retreat down inside the tube, but the shape and construction of their tubes will help you to identify what species lives in them. The larger bristle worms can often be located on the sandy shore by firstly looking for their surface casts or their tubes projecting through the surface of the sand. Otherwise, most will be found by careful digging and sieving of the sediment. They have a variety of forms but the body is usually divided into distinct segments with pairs of paddle-like flaps (**parapodia**) and tiny bristles along the edge. These polychaetes include some species which can move fast, others that tunnel, and those living in permanent or temporary burrows or in a tube. Most tube worms of sandy shores construct their homes from tiny sand grains and fragments of shells (e.g. sand mason worm), whereas those on rocky shores have a hard tube made from calcium carbonate (e.g. keelworm).

You may also encounter other types of worms such as flatworms or ribbon worms on rocky shores.

**CREATURE FEATURES**

- May be free-moving or live in a tube
- A long, soft body composed of many segments
- Only the active burrowers will be found at low tide, tube worms are rarely seen out of water
- Bristles along the sides of the body
- Free-living worms have a head with jaws, sense organs and antennae
- Tube worms often have a crown of feathery tentacles

## Common or estuary ragworm

*Hediste diversicolor*

**Size:** up to 12 cm long
**Colour:** greenish to orange
**Zone:** middle to lower shore
**Habitat:** under stones and in fine muddy sands between boulders, in estuaries, or where fresh water runs over the beach
**Distribution:** widespread
**Field notes:** The ragworm lives in a mucous-lined U or J-shaped burrow up to 20 cm deep. It has a flattened body consisting of 90-120 segments with a bright red blood vessel running the length of the body. The head has 2 eyes, 4 pairs of tentacles and a short **proboscis** with 2 pincer-like jaws. It uses parapodia for crawling and swimming.

## DID YOU KNOW?

The bootlace worm is thought to be the longest living animal. One was recorded as stretching to 55 m long! Although long, the worm is very thin – less than 10 mm wide.

### Bootlace worm

*Lineus longissimus*

**Size:** 5-15 m long but can be over 30 m
**Colour:** very dark brown to black
**Zone:** lower shore
**Habitat:** coiled under rocks and amongst kelp holdfasts or on muddy sand
**Distribution:** widespread
**Field notes:** A type of ribbon worm, the bootlace worm is carnivorous and feeds on polychaete worms. The rectangular head has a row of up to 20 eyes. When handled, the animal produces a large amount of mucus. Ribbon worms do not have segments or bristles.

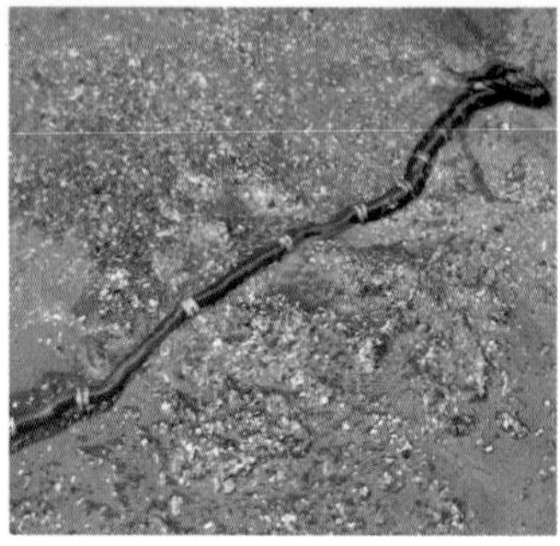

### Football jersey worm

*Tubulanus annulatus*

**Size:** up to 75 cm long and 3-4 mm wide
**Colour:** brick red to brownish marked with 3 white stripes and up to 50 white rings
**Zone:** lower shore
**Habitat:** under stones or on sand and mud
**Distribution:** mainly south west and west coasts of Britain and Ireland
**Field notes:** The football jersey worm is an un-segmented, flattened ribbon worm. It has a broad, rounded head with no visible eyes. This worm is strikingly patterned.

## A scale worm

*Lepidonotus clava*

**Size:** 2-3 cm long
**Colour:** dark brown with some marbling
**Zone:** lower shore
**Habitat:** under boulders
**Distribution:** mainly south and south west coasts of Britain and north east Ireland
**Field notes:** This scale worm has 12 pairs of round scales which do not overlap. The middle of the back is uncovered. There are two pairs of eyes, and bristles along the sides of the body. Several species of scale worm inhabit UK rocky shores, but some can be difficult to identify.

## Candy striped flatworm

*Prostheceraeus vittatus*

**Size:** to 5 cm long
**Colour:** yellow white/cream with dark stripes
**Zone:** lower shore
**Habitat:** under stones
**Distribution:** North Sea, English Channel and Atlantic coasts of Britain and Ireland
**Field notes:** The body is flattened with no segments or bristles. The edge of the body has a wavy appearance as the flatworm glides slowly along. The head has 2 tentacles. At first glance, this flatworm may resemble a sea slug. The candy striped flatworm is carnivorous.

## Green leaf worm

*Eulalia viridis*

**Colour:** bright to dark green
**Zone:** middle to lower shore
**Habitat:** on rocks, in crevices, amongst mussel beds and *Sabellaria* reefs and in kelp holdfasts
**Distribution:** widespread
**Field notes:** The greenleaf worm is a type of paddleworm. It is long and flattened with up to 200 segments. The paddles along the edge of its body are flattened and pointed. The small rounded head has two eyes, and it can extend a long proboscis to catch its prey. It produces green gelatinous egg masses.

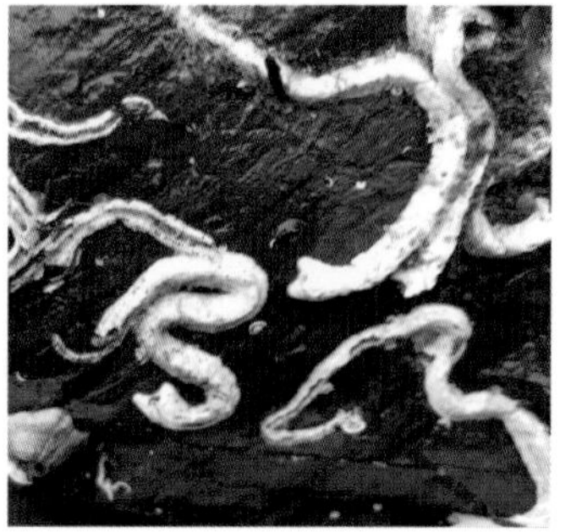

## Keelworm

*Pomatoceros lamarcki*

**Size:** worm is rarely seen at low tide as it is hidden within the tube. Tube is up to 0.5 cm wide and up to 2.5 cm long
**Colour:** tubes are white, worm colour varied
**Zone:** lower shore
**Habitat:** encrusting stones, boulders and shells
**Distribution:** widespread
**Field notes:** The irregularly curved tube is hard and calcareous with a prominent ridge along the top.

## A tubeworm

*Spirobis spirobis*

**Size:** tube is 3 – 4 mm diameter
**Colour:** white tube, worm only shows itself at high tide
**Zone:** middle to lower shore
**Habitat:** on seaweeds such as serrated wrack, bladder wrack and kelps and on stones
**Distribution:** widespread
**Field notes:** The shiny tube is smooth, hard and coils to the left. Large groups of this tubeworm are often found on brown seaweeds, such as serrated wrack, shown in the images.

1. An extensive honeycomb worm reef
2. Close-up of honeycomb worm tubes
3. Turnstone often seen feeding on the honeycomb worm itself

## Honeycomb worm

*Sabellaria alveolata*

**Size:** The reefs built by this tube worm can be several metres across and up to a metre deep. The worm itself is only seen at high tide.
**Colour:** colour of tube varies according to colour of sand grains
**Zone:** lower shore of sand-scoured rocky shores
**Habitat:** in a tube made of sand grains attached to rocks
**Distribution:** limited to south west and western Britain and Ireland
**Field notes:** Each tube is made from strongly cemented sand grains and is rounded 'hexagonal' in section. The honeycomb worm relies on a sand supply to build the tubes, and it may live for 3-5 years. Large reefs or hummocks of worm tubes may be found on the shore. Honeycomb worm reefs are a priority **Biodiversity Action Plan** habitat in the UK. Large reefs provide a valuable habitat for a variety of other species.

6. Animal life

# Sandy shore worms

## Sand mason worm

*Lanice conchilega*

**Size:** worm up to 30 cm long, tube up to 45 cm long
**Colour:** rarely seen at low tide, the worm is pink, yellowish or greenish with white tentacles and red gills, tube sand coloured
**Zone:** middle to lower shore
**Habitat:** in a tube in sand on exposed and sheltered shores
**Distribution:** widespread
**Field notes:** The sand mason worm lives in a tube made of cemented coarse sand grains and shell fragments, with a long fringe or frayed edge around the mouth. The tube can be seen protruding above the sand surface at low tide. It can be found individually or in large populations of several thousand per metre square (see background image).

## Trumpet worm

*Lagis koreni*

**Size:** worm up to 5 cm long, tube up to 8 cm long
**Colour:** worm is white with a pink iridescence and red gills, tube sand coloured
**Zone:** lower shore at very low spring tides
**Habitat:** in a tube in exposed beaches of fine to medium sand
**Distribution:** widespread in Britain and on the north-east Irish coast
**Field notes:** The trumpet worm lives in a smooth, tapering, tusk-shaped or conical tube made of sand grains cemented together. It burrows in the sand, using bundles of spines, with the wider end of the tube pointing downwards and the narrow end angled up to the surface. The trumpet worm feeds on detritus from the sand, and it is eaten by fish such as plaice.

## King Rag worm

*Alitta virens*

**Size:** up to 90 cm long, reaching this length in gravelly and stony areas
**Colour:** dark green with bluish iridescence
**Zone:** lower shore
**Habitat:** burrows in fine muddy sand
**Distribution:** common around Britain and north to north west Ireland
**Field notes:** The body of the king rag consists of up to 175 segments. The edge of the body appears 'frilly' due to the paddles which have a pinkish purple band. The king rag can give a painful bite as it has large jaws. It lives in a mucus-lined burrow and is a good swimmer. King rags are taken from the shore by anglers for bait and also farmed commercially for this.

## Lugworm or Blow lug

*Arenicola marina*

**Size:** up to 20 cm long
**Colour:** pink to dark yellowish green or black
**Zone:** middle to lower shore
**Habitat:** in a burrow in fine to medium sand
**Distribution:** widespread
**Field notes:** The lugworm is a segmented worm with red bushy gills along the middle of its body, a small head and no eyes. It is often used as fishing bait, but is also eaten by many wading birds and flatfish. The lugworm lives in a U-shaped burrow in the sand. The head end is located below the circular depression or 'blow hole' **(1)**, and the tail end below the coiled pile of sand known as a 'worm cast' **(2)**. Approximately every 45 minutes, the lugworm backs up the tail shaft of the burrow to defecate on the surface, leaving the familiar coiled worm cast which looks like squeezed out toothpaste.

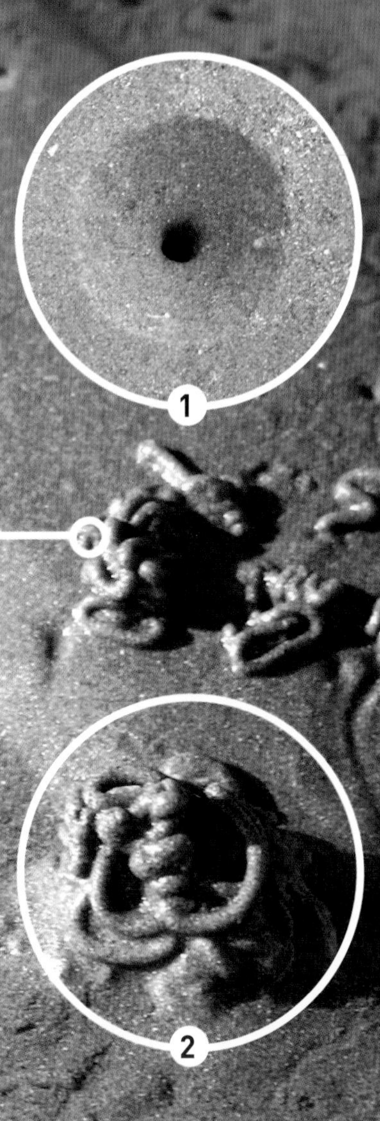

6. Animal life

# Crustaceans

**Crustaceans include barnacles, crabs, lobsters, squat lobsters, prawns and shrimps. They have a wide range of body forms and lifestyles.**

The class **Cirripedia** includes barnacles, whereas the class **Malacostraca** includes crabs, lobsters, prawns and shrimps. The body is generally divided into 3 parts called the head, thorax and abdomen. The legs are jointed and the head appendages include two pairs of antennae and the feeding mouthparts. The shell is called the carapace.

To allow the animal to grow, the exoskeleton is shed or moulted periodically. **Berried** females are those found carrying eggs. On a sandy shore, Crustaceans are represented by several species of crab and shrimp. They are all free-living and actively seek their food. Some live on the sand surface and others bury themselves below or live in burrows.


**Barnacles** **106**
**Crabs and lobsters** **108**
**Prawns and shrimps** **116**
**Sandy shore crabs** **118**

## Angular crab

*Goneplax rhomboides*

**Size:** shell 2 cm across in males, 1.1cm in females
**Colour:** reddish-yellow
**Zone:** lower shore
**Habitat:** muddy sand
**Distribution:** mainly west and south west coasts of Britain and most of Irish coast
**Field notes:** The photograph shows the male angular crab which has very long front pincers or chelipeds, up to 4/5 the length of the shell. The eyes are on long retractable stalks.

### CREATURE FEATURES

- Found in every marine habitat
- Sexes are separate, apart from barnacles which are **hermaphrodite**
- Body divided into head, thorax and abdomen
- Outer body wall made of chitin
- Legs are jointed
- Mostly free-living

# Barnacles

**Barnacles belong to the class Cirripedia. They have a free-swimming minute larval stage in the plankton, which undergoes some changes before becoming adult.**

Young barnacles are free-swimming, but on the shore an adult barnacle is cemented to rocks by its head. It has a shell composed of plates, and feathery legs or **cirri**, used for filter feeding. The cirri can be completely retracted into the shell.

If you look closely at a barnacle in a rockpool, you may be able to watch it extend its feathery legs to catch suspended food particles, drawing them in and out of the shell opening. Barnacles can be difficult to identify with the naked eye. The shape, size and number of outer shell plates are the main identifying features together with the shape of the top opening. A hand lens is needed to see these in detail. Barnacles have many predators including sea snails such as the dog whelk (p.132) and oyster drill (p.131), a sea slug (p.107) and even the Shanny (p.177).

**DID YOU KNOW?**

Groups of small periwinkles can be found living inside empty acorn barnacle shells (p.131). Try to find them using a magnifying lens.

## Volcano barnacle

*Balanus perforatus*

**Size:** up to 5 cm across and 3 cm high
**Colour:** purplish to pink
**Zone:** middle to lower shore
**Habitat:** in shaded areas such as overhangs, attached to rocks
**Distribution:** a southern species found in south west England with its northern limit in south Wales
**Field notes:** A large, tapered, volcano shaped barnacle with an oval opening at the top. The shell consists of 6 plates. Volcano barnacles are being used to monitor climate change. (see page 203).

## Acorn barnacles

The main species occurring on the shore are *Chthamalus montagui, Chthamalus stellatus, Balanus crenatus, Semibalanus balanoides and Austrominius modestus* (non-native from Australia)

**Size:** variable 5 – 20 mm diameter
**Colour:** white to greyish
**Zone:** from upper to lower shore
**Habitat:** attached to rocks
**Distribution:** widespread
**Field notes:** Acorn barnacles cover large areas of open rock surfaces on the rocky shore, and may also be found encrusting mollusc and crustacean shells. British species of barnacles have 6 shell plates. The non-native Australian barnacle has four. The shape of the shell opening ranges from a kite shape to oval or diamond and is an important identification feature. The sea slug *Onchidoris bilamellata* **(1)** feeds entirely on acorn barnacles.

1

# Crabs and lobsters

**Crabs and lobsters belong to the Order Decapoda as they have ten legs. To enable them to grow, crabs must moult their old shells.**

This process is called **ecdysis** and can take a few hours. The shell or **carapace** splits open along a line of weakness across the back, and the body reverses out. The eyes and legs are also pulled out of the old shell. Crabs and lobsters are vulnerable to predation while moulting, and hide away until the new shell hardens in a few days or even weeks. The new body will be about a third bigger than the old one.

Most crabs and lobsters breathe using gills hidden under the shell. The old gills remain in the moulted shell and new ones grow (page 113). If they lose a leg or claw, they can regenerate a new one. This forms inside the shell and is exposed at the next moult. Hermit crabs, however, are a special case as they do not have their own shells (page 113). The front claws or pincers have different jobs. One is for cutting and one is for crushing.

## KEY FEATURES

- Body divided into 3 segmented regions: head, thorax, abdomen with additional tail or telson
- Head appendages modified as antennae, mouthparts and feeding structures
- Thorax appendages modified for walking and swimming
- Outer body wall or **exoskeleton** made of chitin
- Growth requires periodic moulting involving shedding the exoskeleton and growing a new, larger shell
- 5 pairs of legs
- Two large front pincers or **chelipeds**

### Hairy crab

*Pilumnus hirtellus*

**Size:** shell up to 1.5 cm across
**Colour:** brownish red or purplish, legs banded purple/cream
**Zone:** lower shore
**Habitat:** on rock and stony bottoms in pools and under boulders
**Distribution:** widespread but most frequent in the south and west of Britain
**Field notes:** There are 5 sharp teeth on either side of the carapace. The pincers are large and very unequal. The shell and all of the walking legs are covered in hairs.

## Long-legged spider crab

*Macropodia rostrata*

**Size:** shell up to 2.2 cm long
**Colour:** brown tinged with grey, yellow or red
**Zone:** lower shore
**Habitat:** under seaweeds or boulders
**Distribution:** widespread except in western Ireland
**Field notes:** The long-legged spider crab is very well camouflaged, with pieces of red seaweed often attached to its body. The legs are long and slender.

### DID YOU KNOW?

Male crabs have a narrow 'v' shaped tail with 5 joints and in females the tail is wider with 7 joints. You can see this by turning the crab over carefully.

## Risso's crab

*Xantho pilipes*

**Size:** up to 3 cm long
**Colour:** yellowish with patches of red.
**Zone:** lower shore
**Habitat:** under rocks and boulders
**Distribution:** western coasts of Britain up to Shetland, on the south west coast, and most of Ireland
**Field notes:** Risso's crab has a dense layer of hairs on the carapace and on the walking legs. This is a key feature in distinguishing it from the furrowed crab. The large pincers have brown tips.

## Velvet swimming crab, Fiddler crab or Devil crab

*Necora puber*

**Size:** shell up 8 cm across
**Colour:** shell blue with brown velvety covering
**Zone:** middle to lower shore
**Habitat:** under rocks, boulders and seaweeds
**Distribution:** widespread
**Field notes:** The velvet swimming crab is characterised by its red eyes, bright blue lines on the legs and claws and flattened paddle-like back legs. It is fast moving and defends itself aggressively with its powerful pincers. There are 5 pointed teeth on the edge of the shell, either side of the eyes.

## Furrowed or Montagu's crab

*Xantho incisus*

**Size:** shell up to 2.5 cm long and 6 cm wide
**Colour:** yellowish-green to reddish-brown
**Zone:** lower shore
**Habitat:** under rocks and boulders
**Distribution:** south and west coasts of Britain and west coast of Ireland.
**Field notes:** There are thick 'wrinkles' or furrows along the shell. It is similar to Risso's crab, but does not have any hairs on the body. The large pincers have black tips.

## Leach's spider crab

*Inachus phalangium*

**Size:** shell up to 2 cm long
**Colour:** brownish red
**Zone:** lower shore
**Habitat:** often at the base of a snakelocks anemone or on coarse sediment
**Distribution:** widespread
**Field notes:** Leach's spider crab is well camouflaged, often with sponge attached to its body (orange blotches shown on image). The surfaces of the triangular shell and long slender legs are covered in hook-like hairs.

## Common or Spiny spider crab

*Maja squinado*

**Size:** shell up to 20 cm long, front pincers up to 45 cm long
**Colour:** shell red, brownish or orange
**Zone:** lower shore
**Habitat:** under seaweeds, and in deep rockpools
**Distribution:** common off west and south west coasts of Britain
**Field notes:** The shell is rough and covered in spines and often sponges, barnacles, hydroids and seaweeds. This helps to camouflage it.

## Edible or Brown crab

*Cancer pagurus*

**Size:** up to 25 cm wide in large males
**Colour:** reddish-brown, with black tips to front pincers
**Zone:** middle to lower shore
**Habitat:** under rocks and boulders, under seaweeds, in crevices
**Distribution:** widespread
**Field notes:** The edible crab is commonly called the 'pasty crab' because of the pie-crust edge to its oval shell. It is the largest crab likely to be seen on the shore. Large males can live for more than 20 to 100 years. The edible crab in the picture above has just moulted its old shell shown in the insert **(1)**. If you look closely, you can see that the old gills either side of the shell have been left behind. The edible crab's new shell is soft and so it is hiding away in a crevice until it hardens.

1

## Common hermit crab

*Pagurus bernhardus*

**Size:** up to 3.5 cm
**Colour:** orange to reddish body
**Zone:** middle to lower shore
**Habitat:** in rockpools
**Distribution:** widespread
**Field notes:** Unlike other crabs, a hermit crab does not have its own shell and so it lives in any empty sea snail shell, especially those of the common whelk.
It has a soft unprotected body, which is coiled to fit the coils of a shell. As it grows and moults, it discards its old shell and backs its body into a new, larger shell. It is very vulnerable to predation at this time. Only the head end, legs and front claws are usually seen poking out of the adopted shell. The head and legs are covered with small spiny projections and bristles. The right-hand pincer is the larger and is used to close the shell entrance when the hermit crab is hiding inside. It scavenges on dead plant and animal remains.

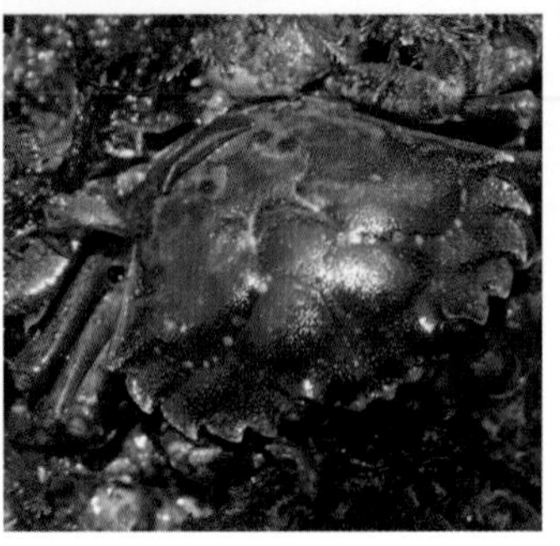

## Common shore crab

*Carcinus maenas*

**Size:** shell up to 8 cm across
**Colour:** variable, mottled dark green to orange or brownish
**Zone:** middle to lower shore
**Habitat:** under stones, under seaweeds, in crevices, in rockpools, on sandy shores and along estuaries
**Distribution:** widespread
**Field notes:** This is our most common seashore crab. There are 5 teeth on the shell either side of the eyes, and 3 rounded lobes between the eyes. During the winter, the common shore crab moves offshore.

## Broad-clawed porcelain crab

*Porcellana platycheles*

**Size:** shell length up to 1.5 cm long
**Colour:** greyish brown above, yellowish white underneath
**Zone:** middle to lower shore
**Habitat:** undersides of boulders
**Distribution:** widespread
**Field notes:** The broad-clawed porcelain crab is covered in fine hairs, and has wide, flat claws and long antennae. The claws hold the crab tightly to the rock surface. Only 3 pairs of walking legs are visible. The others are much reduced and tucked up underneath.

## Squat lobster

*Galathea squamifera*

**Size:** up to 6.5 cm long
**Colour:** dark brown with greenish blue tinge
**Zone:** lower shore
**Habitat:** under rocks and boulders and in crevices
**Distribution:** most coasts of Britain and Ireland
**Field notes:** The squat lobster feeds on suspended matter. It has long front pincers, and the tail is tucked tightly underneath the body. It is not a true lobster.

## Common lobster

*Homarus gammarus*

**Size:** up to 50 cm long
**Colour:** bright blue above, yellowish below, red antennae
**Zone:** lower shore
**Habitat:** under boulders, in rockpools, in crevices and under overhangs
**Distribution:** widespread
**Field notes:** The common lobster can live for 15 to 20 years or more. The pincers are large and very powerful, and are unequal in size. Lobsters should be handled with care. Note: this lobster has lost its right pincer.

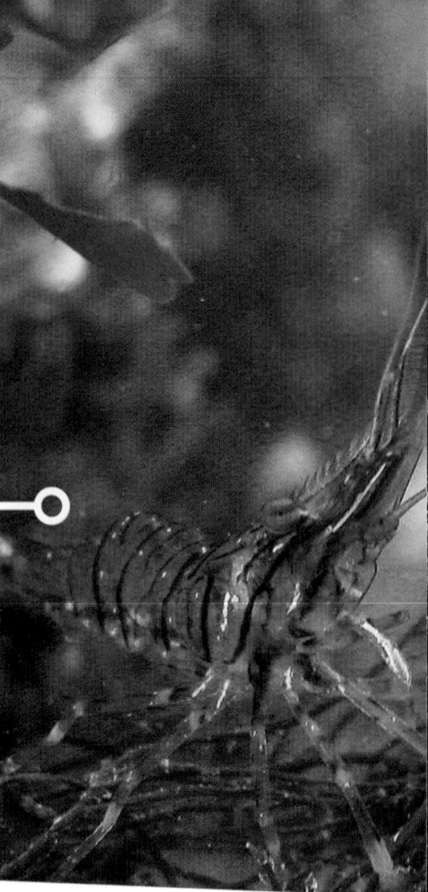

**Common prawn**
*Palaemon serratus*
**Size:** up to 11 cm long
**Colour:** transparent with red/brown lines and blue, red and yellow striped front legs
**Zone:** upper to lower shore
**Habitat:** in rockpools, in crevices, under overhangs and under rocks and boulders
**Distribution:** widespread
**Field notes:** The common prawn has large eyes. It can move very quickly. Prawns are very inquisitive and if you stand in a rockpool and keep still and quiet, they will readily approach your feet.



# Prawns and shrimps

**Prawns and shrimps have two pairs of feeding legs, five pairs of swimming legs and ten walking legs.**

They have very small pincers on the front legs, used to collect food including pieces of seaweeds, dead creatures and small live prey. Their eyes are on stalks. There are two pairs of antennae, one pair usually being very long.

When frightened, they suddenly shoot backwards by flipping the tail, and hide under seaweed or stones.

Prawns and shrimps are an important link in the food chain of a rocky shore, as they feed on waste matter or detritus, and they in turn are eaten by many fish and bird species (see page 25).

## Brown shrimp

*Crangon crangon*

**Size:** up to 9 cm
**Colour:** grey to sandy brown with darker spots or mottled
**Zone:** middle shore to lower shore
**Habitat:** on fine muddy sands and gravels and in pools
**Distribution:** widespread
**Field notes:** The brown shrimp is very well camouflaged and is often buried, with only the eyes and antennae visible above the sand surface. The main antennae are nearly as long as the body and the tail is fan-shaped.

## Chameleon prawn

*Hippolyte varians*

**Size:** up to 2.5 cm long
**Colour:** variable depending on the background, often green, red or brown in day and transparent at night
**Zone:** lower shore
**Habitat:** amongst rocks and seaweeds in rockpools and gullies
**Distribution:** widespread
**Field notes:** As its name suggests, the chameleon prawn can change colour **(1)** to match its surroundings. It has a spine above each eye.

1

# Sandy shore crabs

## Masked crab

*Corystes cassivelaunus*

**Size:** shell up to 4 cm long
**Colour:** pale red to yellowish-white
**Zone:** lower shore
**Habitat:** burrows in fine sand
**Distribution:** a Southern species found on many British and Irish coasts
**Field notes:** When the masked crab is buried, the pair of long antennae form a tube up to the surface, down which clean oxygenated water is funnelled to its gills. It can often be found with just its eyes above the sand surface and its long antennae sticking up **(1)**. The pincers of the male are twice as long as the shell. There are ridges on the shell which look like a face.

## Pennant's swimming crab

*Portumnus latipes*

**Size:** shell up to 2 cm long
**Colour:** reddish brown with white patches
**Zone:** lower shore
**Habitat:** burrows in the top few layers of sand
**Distribution:** scattered locations in Britain, mainly south west England and Wales
**Field notes:** Pennant's swimming crab is a small and flat crab with a heart-shaped, smooth carapace or shell. It has 3 blunt lobes between the eyes and 5 teeth either side of the eyes.

## South-claw or small hermit crab

*Diogenes pugilator*

**Size:** carapace may reach up to 1.1 cm in length
**Colour:** yellowish-green
**Zone:** lower shore
**Habitat:** in sand on sheltered sandy coasts
**Distribution:** the south western coasts of Britain as far north as Anglesey and the south and west coasts of Ireland
**Field notes:** The south-claw hermit crab differs from most other hermit crabs by having a left claw considerably larger than the right. Both claws are covered in minute hairs. Image **(2)** shows the south-claw hermit crab rapidly burrowing in the sand, to escape predators.

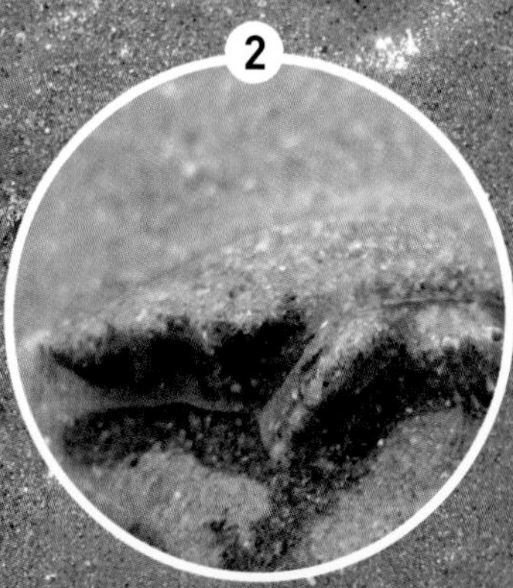

6. Animal life

# Molluscs

**Molluscs are one of the largest groups of marine organisms, and include chitons, sea snails, sea slugs and bivalves.**

Most have a soft, fleshy body and a strong muscular foot.
The head has eyes and tentacles. Molluscs may or may not have a shell which is secreted by part of the body called the mantle. The shell is strengthened by calcium carbonate crystals.

They are free-living animals and are very variable in form and in their methods of feeding.

Most **molluscs** (apart from bivalves), have a ribbon of teeth called the radula, used to scrape up food and transport it to be digested in the body. The radula teeth are replaced continually.

These animals have gills which are used for breathing. Molluscs are some of the main inhabitants of a sandy shore.


| | |
|---|---|
| **Chitons** | **122** |
| **Sea snails** | **124** |
| **Sea slugs** | **136** |
| **Bivalves** | **142** |

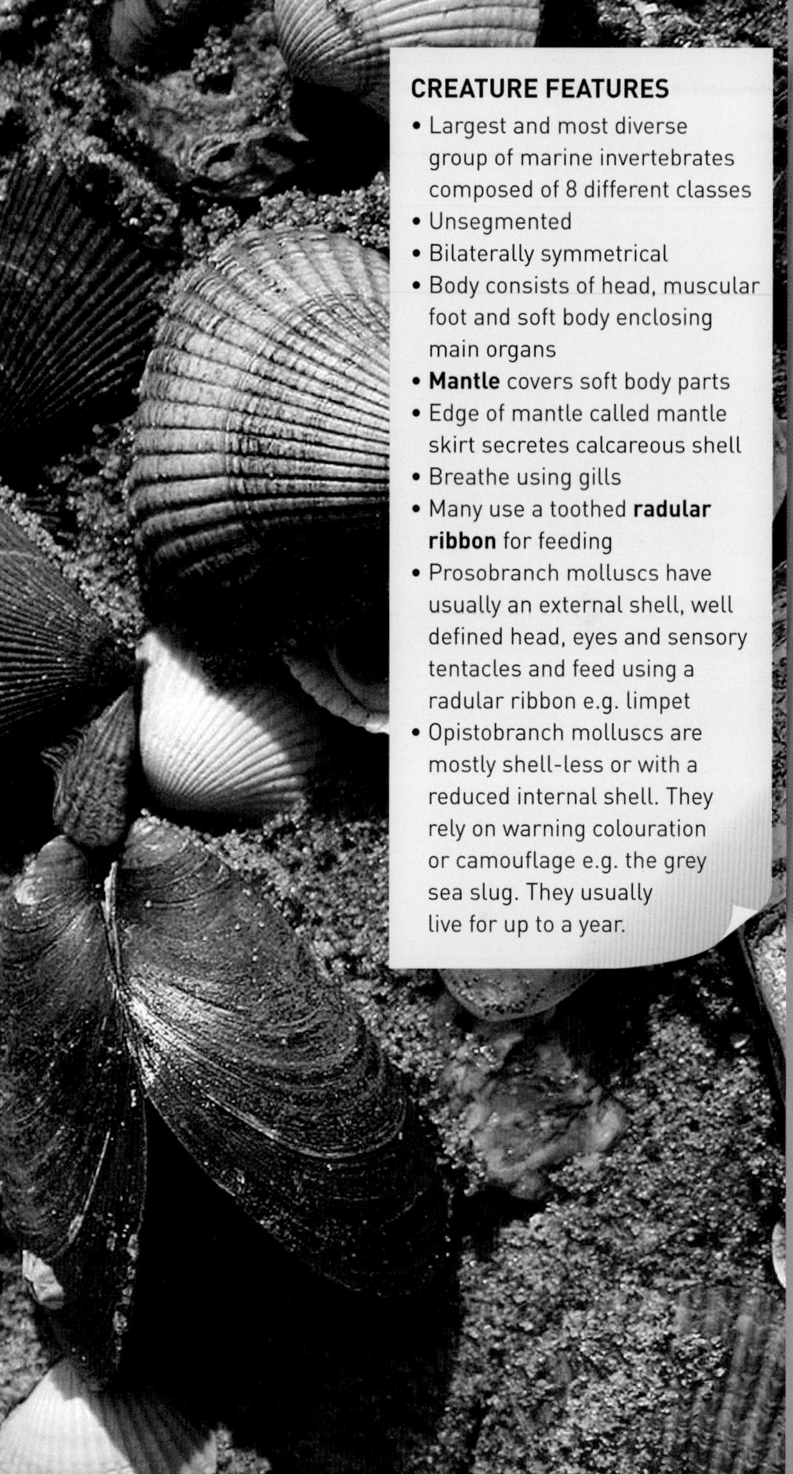

## CREATURE FEATURES

- Largest and most diverse group of marine invertebrates composed of 8 different classes
- Unsegmented
- Bilaterally symmetrical
- Body consists of head, muscular foot and soft body enclosing main organs
- **Mantle** covers soft body parts
- Edge of mantle called mantle skirt secretes calcareous shell
- Breathe using gills
- Many use a toothed **radular ribbon** for feeding
- Prosobranch molluscs have usually an external shell, well defined head, eyes and sensory tentacles and feed using a radular ribbon e.g. limpet
- Opistobranch molluscs are mostly shell-less or with a reduced internal shell. They rely on warning colouration or camouflage e.g. the grey sea slug. They usually live for up to a year.

# Chitons

**Chitons are also called coat-of-mail shells because of the appearance of the shell, which looks as if it is made of links of chain mail.**

The shell is composed of eight arched **plates** which fit very closely together. This helps them to bend and cling to uneven rock surfaces, using a large muscular foot. The body is oval shaped, and chitons can curl up into a ball like a woodlouse. They feed using a radula, and scrape off and eat microscopic algae growing on the rocks.

Chitons are predated by crabs and fish. They are difficult to identify, and may look like tiny fossils at first glance, but are actually living creatures. They are only found on rocky shores.

### A chiton

*Acanthochitona crinita*

**Size:** up to 3 cm long
**Colour:** brown-yellow, pinkish or marbled
**Zone:** lower shore
**Habitat:** on underside of rocks
**Distribution:** mainly on west and south west coasts of Britain and Ireland
**Field notes:** This species of chiton has 18 evenly spaced tufts of rough bristles around the edge of the shell plates.

### A chiton

*Tonicella rubra*

**Size:** up to 2 cm long
**Colour:** marbled brown and white/reddish
**Zone:** lower shore
**Habitat:** on rocks
**Distribution:** widespread around British Isles but only on north east Irish coast
**Field notes:** The edge of the shell is fringed with tiny, flat spines.

## A chiton

*Lepidochitona cinerea*

**Size:** up to 2.5 cm long
**Colour:** variable with alternating light and dark bands
**Zone:** lower shore
**Habitat:** on rocks
**Distribution:** widespread
**Field notes:** The shell is oval-shaped, with tiny nodules and short spines on the outer edge. *Lepidochitona cinerea* is the most commonly found chiton species in the intertidal zone.

# Sea snails

**Sea snails or gastropods are classed as Prosobranch molluscs. They have a single, hard outer shell comprising a series of whorls.**

The shell shape can be very variable, from a small cone to a long spindle. The shell colour is also very variable and it can be crossed by ridges and growth lines. Sea snails can pull their body into the shell and close the entrance with a horny disc called the operculum (see page 129, image 2). At low tide, this prevents the soft bodied animal from drying out and protects it. They have a strong foot which helps them burrow and it may also be lobed to enable them to plough through the soft sediment of sandy shores. They have a definite head end with tentacles and some breathe air using a lung. Sea snails live on rocky and sandy shores.

## Spotted or European Cowrie

*Trivia monacha*

**Size:** shell up to 1.2 cm long
**Colour:** shell pinkish with 3 dark spots, head, tentacles, foot and mantle are brightly coloured often orange or red
**Zone:** lower shore
**Habitat:** under overhangs, under and on boulders, in crevices
**Distribution:** widespread but mainly west coast of Britain and Ireland
**Field notes:** The spotted cowrie has three dark spots/blotches on its back and a ridged shell. It has a bright orange foot and two head tentacles. The mantle almost covers the shell when moving. It looks like fake leopard-skin. The photograph opposite clearly shows this, together with the tentacles and siphon on the head and the foot underneath. The insert above shows two spotted cowries under a boulder. The preferred food of the cowrie are colonial sea squirts (p.169).

## Arctic or northern cowrie

*Trivia arctica*

**Size:** shell 1 cm long and 8 mm wide
**Colour:** pale pink-white
**Zone:** lower shore
**Habitat:** under boulders
**Distribution:** mainly north and west coasts of Britain and around Ireland
**Field notes:** The Arctic cowrie is similar to the Spotted cowrie, but it is paler, has no spots, and is usually smaller. There are thick ridges running along the oval shell. It feeds on ascidians such as the star sea squirt (p.170).

## Common keyhole limpet

*Diodora graeca*

**Size:** shell up to 4 cm long
**Colour:** body white or greyish, but may be yellow, orange or red
**Zone:** lower shore
**Habitat:** on rocks
**Distribution:** western Britain, southern England and widespread around Ireland
**Field notes:** The common keyhole limpet is a sea snail which feeds on sponges, especially breadcrumb sponge. The shell is a low cone shape with radiating ridges, and a hole at the top used for respiration.

## Blue-rayed limpet

*Ansates pellucida*

**Size:** up to 1.5 cm long
**Colour:** shell translucent amber with brilliant kingfisher blue lines
**Zone:** lower shore
**Habitat:** almost entirely on fronds and stipes of large kelps
**Distribution:** widespread
**Field notes:** The blue-rayed limpet has a strikingly coloured shell marked with kingfisher-blue lines. The shell is small and oval shaped. This species excavates a groove on kelp, in which it lives **(1)**. It also grazes on the seaweed. It can live for 1-2 years.

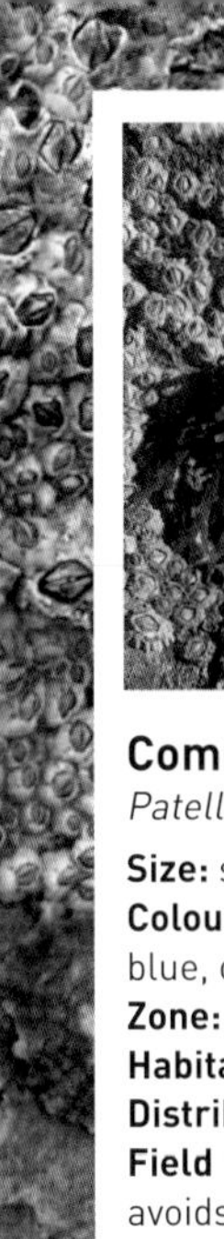

## Common limpet

*Patella vulgata*

**Size:** shell up to 6 cm long
**Colour:** shell grey or greenish-blue, often covered in barnacles
**Zone:** upper shore downwards
**Habitat:** on rocks
**Distribution:** widespread
**Field notes:** The common limpet avoids drying out at low tide by clamping down on rocks with its muscular foot. Common limpets can live for 15-20 years. On the upper shore, the shell is steeply conical, and on the lower shore, it is much flatter. This helps it to survive strong wave action, especially on more exposed shores. There are two other British *Patella* species i.e. *P. ulyssiponensis* (China limpet) and *P. depressa* (Black-footed limpet). They are difficult to tell apart. The common limpet is the species most often encountered. Try searching on rocks for its zig zag grazing pattern **(2)**.

### DID YOU KNOW?

At high tide, limpets leave their places on the rocks and feed on the thin layer of young seaweeds covering the rocks. They have a home range of about 3 metres. When the tide drops, they return to their exact starting place on the rocks, by following a fine slime trail. This place is called the home scar and is created by grinding the shell into the rock until it is a perfect fit. The background image shows some home scars but not all the limpets will return, as they may be predated by seabirds or dog whelks, or dislodged by waves.

## Toothed or Thick top shell

*Osilinus lineatus*

**Size:** shell up to 3 cm high
**Colour:** dark green, grey or black, with brown or red zigzags
**Zone:** middle shore
**Habitat:** in rockpools and on open rocks
**Distribution:** south and west coasts of Britain and Ireland. Absent from Scotland and eastern England
**Field notes:** The toothed top shell has 'mother of pearl' inside the shell opening and a distinctive 'tooth' on the inside of the mouth opening **(1)**.

## Grey top shell

*Gibbula cineraria*

**Size:** shell up to 1.5 cm high
**Colour:** ash grey with thin reddish brown curved bands
**Zone:** middle to lower shore
**Habitat:** on sheltered rocky shores on seaweed, and under rocks or in rockpools
**Distribution:** widespread
**Field notes:** The grey top shell has a shell which is blunt and conical with 5 to 6 **whorls**. The shell has fine spiral ridges and grooves.

## Flat or purple top shell

*Gibbula umbilicalis*

**Size:** shell up to 1.5 cm high
**Colour:** dull greenish with broad stripes of reddish-purple
**Zone:** middle to lower shore
**Habitat:** on sheltered rocky shores
**Distribution:** mainly on western shores of the UK and Ireland
**Field notes:** The flat top shell can live for up to 10 years. There is a conspicuous circular hole on the underside of the shell called the **umbilicus**. The shell is a flattish cone shape with up to 7 whorls.

## Painted top shell

*Calliostoma zizyphinum*

**Size:** shell up to 3 cm high and 3 cm wide
**Colour:** shell pinkish purple with blotches, or sometimes white. The animal is often orange.
**Zone:** lower shore from mid tide level
**Habitat:** on rocks and under overhangs
**Distribution:** widespread
**Field notes:** The painted top shell is our most colourful top shell. It has a coiled cone-shaped shell like a spinning top, with spiral grooves and ridges. Image **(2)** below shows the underside and the operculum which is used to close the shell.

### DID YOU KNOW?

Top shells can be indicators of climate change (see page 203).

## Flat periwinkle

*Littorina obtusata*

**Size:** up to 1.5 cm high
**Colour:** varies according to habitat from green, orange, yellow, brown or black
**Zone:** middle to lower shore
**Habitat:** on large brown seaweeds such as bladder wrack and egg wrack
**Distribution:** widespread
**Field notes:** The head tentacles of the flat periwinkle have two lines along them. It feeds on brown seaweeds like bladder wrack and can be mistaken for the actual bladders **(1)**. It lays jelly-like egg masses on brown seaweed and can live for about three years. The shell is oval shaped, quite smooth and has a flat top and a very small spire.

## Common or Edible periwinkle

*Littorina littorea*

**Size:** shell up to 3 cm high
**Colour:** black to dark grey-brown, sometimes red or white
**Zone:** upper to lower shore
**Habitat:** on rocks
**Distribution:** widespread
**Field notes:** In the common periwinkle, the head tentacles have many black stripes running across them and one line along them. The shell is the largest of the periwinkles and has a small pointed spire and fine grooves on the surface. Like all periwinkles, this animal is a herbivore.
The egg capsules are shed directly into the sea, and on hatching, the larvae become part of the plankton.

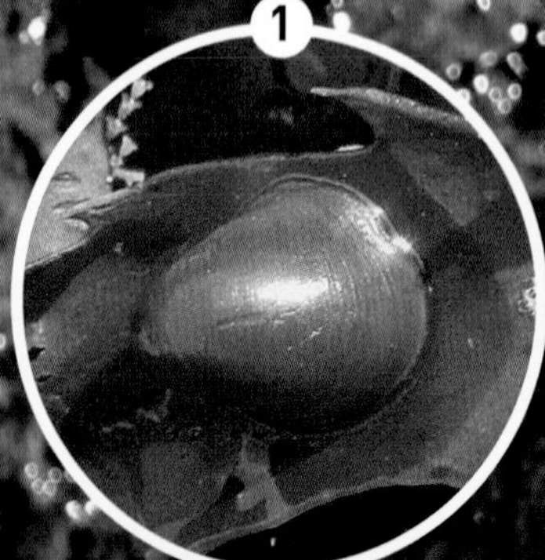

## Rough periwinkle

*Littorina saxatilis*

**Size:** shell up to 2 cm high
**Colour:** variable
**Zone:** upper shore
**Habitat:** amongst channelled and spiral wracks, in crevices and on rocks
**Distribution:** widespread
**Field notes:** The rough periwinkle has a small shell with 3-4 whorls and ridges.

## Oyster drill or European sting winkle

*Ocenebra erinacea*

**Size:** shell up to 5 cm long
**Colour:** shell cream with brown patches
**Zone:** lower shore
**Habitat:** on rocks and under stones and in silty crevices
**Distribution:** mainly west and south west coasts of Britain and around Ireland
**Field notes:** The oyster drill preys on cockles, other molluscs and barnacles. It uses the radula, and acid-producing glands on the sole of the foot, to break through their shells. The shell of the oyster drill is very ridged and sharply pointed, with about 5 whorls.

## Small periwinkle

*Melarhaphe neritoides*

**Size:** shell less than 1 cm high
**Colour:** black or dark brown
**Zone:** splash zone to upper shore
**Habitat:** in empty barnacle shells (shown above) and in crevices
**Distribution:** western coasts of Britain
**Field notes:** The tiny small periwinkle has a shell with a small, pointed spire. The head tentacles have two dark lines running down them.

## Dog whelk

*Nucella lapillus*

**Size:** shell around 4 cm high
**Colour:** variable, white to dark brown, yellow or banded **(1)**
**Zone:** middle shore downwards
**Habitat:** on rocks, under overhangs and in crevices
**Distribution:** widespread
**Field notes:** Female lays yellow flask-shaped capsules on rocks. Each capsule **(2)** contains several hundred eggs, but not all will be fertile. The dog whelk is a predator, using its radula to drill into the shell of mussels and barnacles. Its digestive juices dissolve the prey and it uses its proboscis to suck up its food. The shell shape varies with wave exposure. Dog whelks can live for 5-10 years.

1

## Necklace shell

*Polinices catenus*

**Size:** up to 3 cm high
**Colour:** buff to pale yellow
**Zone:** lower shore
**Habitat:** buried in sheltered to moderately exposed sand
**Distribution:** widespread
**Field notes:** The necklace shell is similar to alder's necklace shell but it is larger and paler in colour. It feeds on small bivalves such as the banded wedge shell by drilling a round hole through the shell **(1)**. There is a single spiral row of brown marks near to the upper shell edge. It uses its large lobed foot to plough through the sand **(2)**. Egg capsules are laid in a horseshoe shaped egg collar made of a mass of jelly and sand grains **(3)**.

## Netted or reticulated dog whelk

*Hinia reticulata*

**Size:** shell up to 3 cm long
**Colour:** brownish with dark bands
**Zone:** lower shore
**Habitat:** on muddy areas between rocks and in crevices
**Distribution:** widespread
**Field notes:** The netted dog whelk can be found buried in soft sediment with just the siphon protruding. It lays flat egg capsules attached to seaweeds and rocks.

## Common whelk

*Buccinum undatum*

**Size:** Up to 10 cm high and 6 cm wide
**Colour:** body of animal yellow-white with black flecks, shell yellowish brown
**Zone:** lower shore
**Habitat:** on muddy sand
**Distribution:** all British coasts
**Field notes:** Has a ridged shell with 7 – 8 whorls. The empty egg masses are often found on the strandline and are called 'sea wash balls' (see page 75).

## Alder's necklace shell

*Polinices pulchellus*

**Size:** up to 1.6 cm high and 1.2 cm wide
**Colour:** 5 spiral rows of brown markings
**Zone:** lower shore
**Habitat:** buried in sheltered to moderately exposed sand
**Distribution:** widespread
**Field notes:** Alder's necklace shell is glossy and smooth with a large aperture. There are 5 distinctive rows of brown markings on the shell. The large foot has two long flattened tentacles. It feeds on bivalves, especially tellins. The egg capsules are laid in a circular egg collar on sand in spring and early summer. Like the necklace shell, alder's necklace shell can be found ploughing through the top layers of sand, leaving a deep trail.

# Sea slugs

**Sea slugs are classed as Opistobranch molluscs and are some of the most fascinating and brightly coloured animals found on the rocky shore.**

They may or may not have a shell. They often have a ring of feathery external gills towards the rear end, and can be many shapes and sizes. The distinct head has a pair of tentacles called **rhinophores**, the shape of which can help in identification. The sea hare is a type of **sacoglossan** as it has an internal shell and is a **herbivore**. All of the other sea slugs outlined here are called **nudibranchs** as they have no shell and extremely varied shapes. They are mainly carnivorous. Nudibranchs often have skin glands which produce toxins, making them unpalatable to predators. Some feed on sea anemones or hydroids, using the stinging cells as their own defence mechanism by storing them in feathery or bulbous projections called **cerata**.

All **opistobranchs** are hermaphrodite and the eggs or spawn are laid in different coloured, shaped and sized ribbons or capsules, depending on the species (see image below). Several types of sea slug can be found on a sandy shore. Most are infaunal and prey on worms and bivalves. Unlike most rocky shore sea slug species, those of sandy shores have external shells. These can often be found along the strandline.

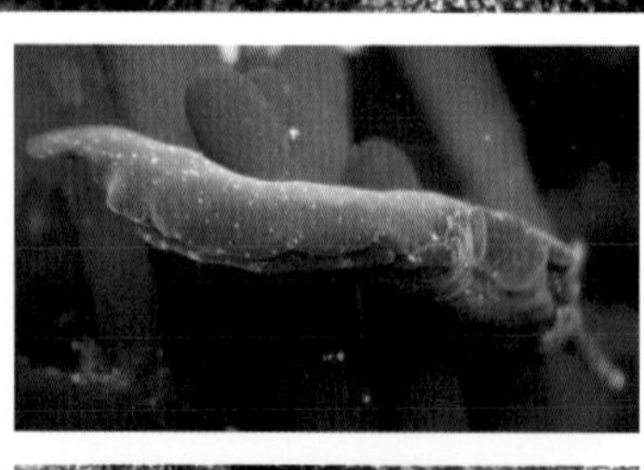

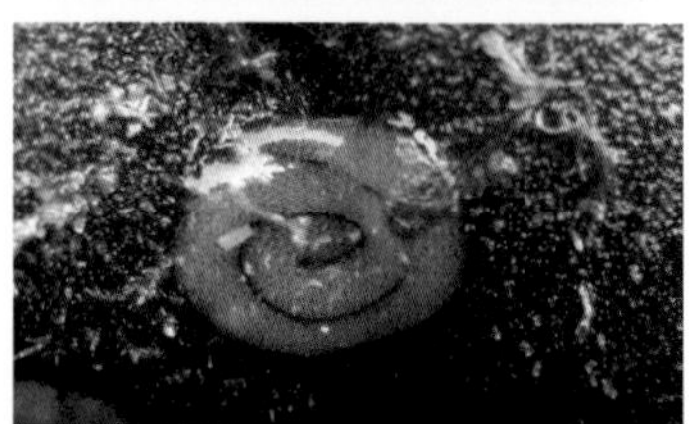

## A sea slug

*Elysia viridis*

**Size:** up to 4.5 cm long
**Colour:** vivid green with bright blue and green spots
**Zone:** lower shore
**Habitat:** on seaweeds especially species of *Codium* and in rockpools
**Distribution:** widespread
**Field notes:** *Elysia viridis* eats green algae and ingests the chloroplasts which contain the green pigment chlorophyll hence its bright green colour. It lays coils of spawn on seaweed (shown in lower image).

## Sea hare

*Aplysia punctata*

**Size:** body commonly between 7 and 10 cm long
**Colour:** olive-green, brown or purplish black in adults
**Zone:** lower shore
**Habitat:** rock pools with seaweed
**Distribution:** widespread
**Field notes:** The sea hare is a large sea slug with an internal shell and two pairs of tentacles on the head. It can be found in rockpools, grazing on seaweeds especially sea lettuce and kelp. It can produce an ink-like dye to deter predators.

## A sea slug

*Facelina auriculata*

**Size:** up to 3.8 cm
**Colour:** translucent white with pink tint and blue iridescence
**Zone:** lower shore
**Habitat:** under boulders and on hydroids and kelps
**Distribution:** widespread except in south east Britain
**Field notes:** This sea slug has a blue iridescence on its head and body and feeds on hydroids (sea firs). The mouth tentacles are very long.

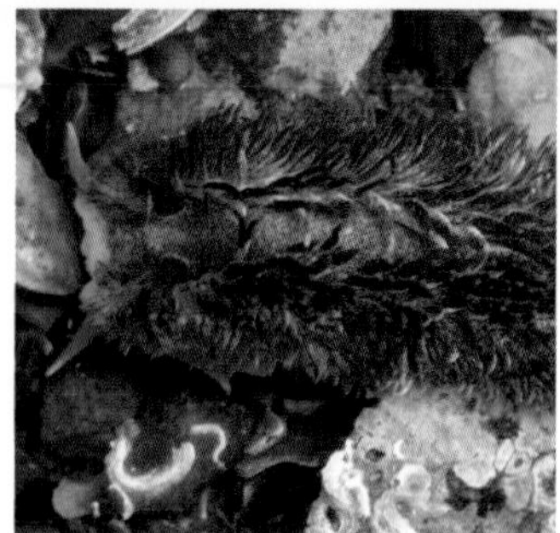

## Grey sea slug

*Aeolidia papillosa*

**Size:** up to 12 cm long
**Colour:** variable: cream, brown, grey, orange-pink, dark purple-brown
**Zone:** middle to lower shore
**Habitat:** under rocks and in rockpools
**Distribution:** widespread
**Field notes:** Although commonly called the grey sea slug, it can be many other colours (see above and page 51). It is a large sea slug covered in a dense layer of 'furry' cerata. There is a distinctive 'V' shaped patch on the front of the head.

## A sea slug

*Aeolidiella alderi*

**Size:** up to 4.5 cm
**Colour:** yellowish
**Zone:** lower shore
**Habitat:** rockpools
**Distribution:** scattered locations in east and north west Scotland, south and south west England and north and south Ireland
**Field notes:** This sea slug looks a bit like the grey sea slug but can be distinguished by a ruff of white cerata behind the head. It feeds on a variety of sea anemones.

## Sea lemon

*Archidoris pseudoargus*

**Size:** up to 7 cm long
**Colour:** variable blotchy colour pattern, often yellow, orange or brown
**Zone:** lower shore
**Habitat:** under large boulders and under overhangs
**Distribution:** widespread

**Field notes:** The Sea lemon is the commonest and most familiar sea slug on our shores. It feeds on encrusting sponges such as breadcrumb sponge. The top of the animal is covered in small 'warts' called **tubercles** and it secretes poison from glands in the skin to protect itself. The insert **(1)** shows a Sea lemon out of water under an overhang.

## A sea slug

*Acteon tornatilis*

**Size:** up to 2-3 cm long
**Colour:** banded glossy pink and white shell
**Zone:** middle to lower shore
**Habitat:** burrows in fine sand and sandy muds
**Distribution:** scattered locations around Britain and Ireland
**Field notes:** This primitive shelled sea slug is a carnivore. It feeds on sand mason worms, which may take up to two hours to devour. It can live for more than 5 years. It leaves deep trails in the sand surface as it travels along searching for prey (see background image), and is often active at low tide. It may cover 10 metres or more. The whole of the body can be withdrawn into the shell.

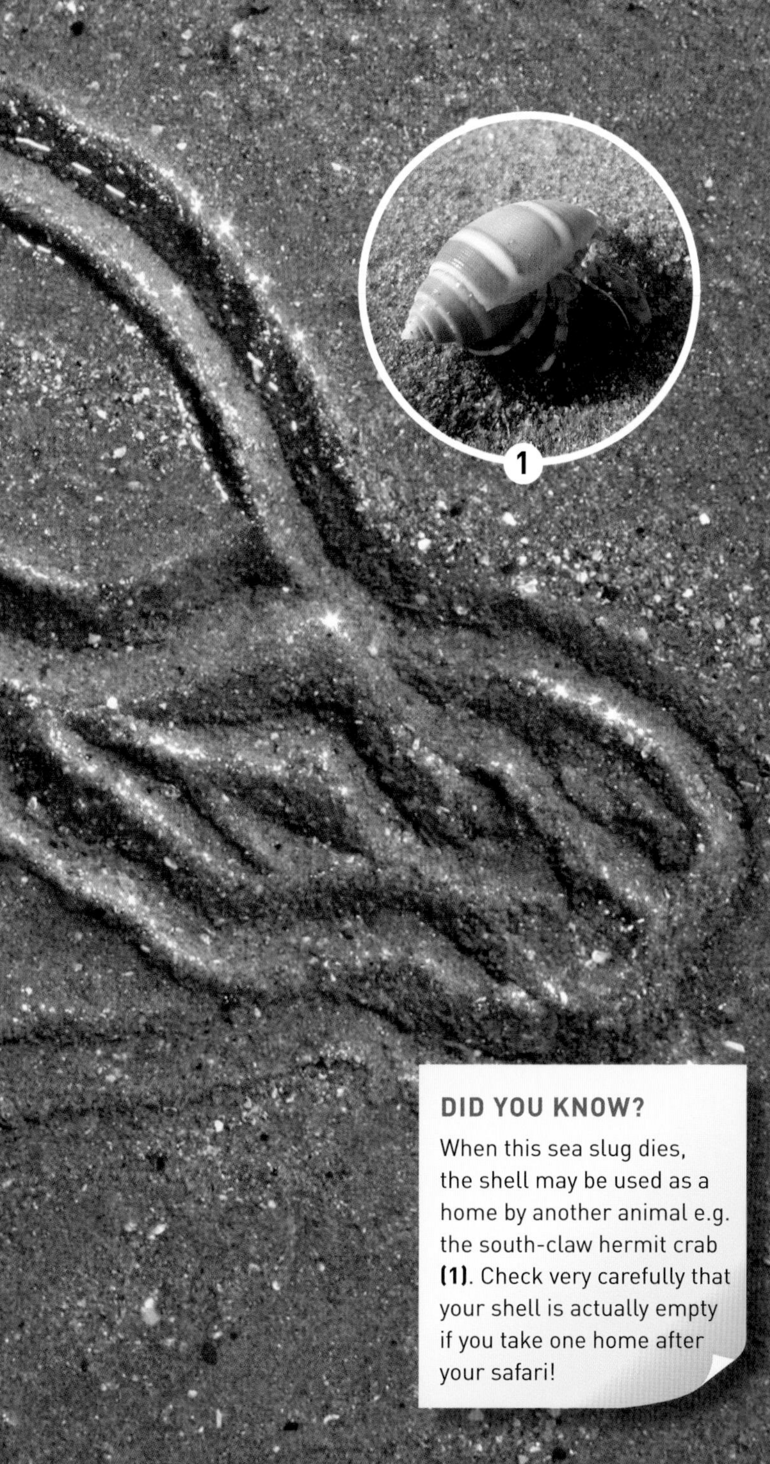


**DID YOU KNOW?**

When this sea slug dies, the shell may be used as a home by another animal e.g. the south-claw hermit crab **(1)**. Check very carefully that your shell is actually empty if you take one home after your safari!

# Bivalves

**Bivalve molluscs belong to the Class Pelecypoda and have two shells or valves joined together by a ligament and hinge. This hard shell protects the soft body inside. They have powerful muscles which are used to open and shut the valves.**

Bivalves attach themselves to rocks by **byssus** threads, bore into rocks or burrow in sediment. When the tide is in, they feed, breathe and eject waste products by extending two tubes or siphons to the water or sediment surface. They have internal gills. They are filter feeders, and have no head or radula. Shallow and deep burrowing species of bivalve are often abundant on sandy shores, except for very exposed beaches. They use a strong muscular foot to pull themselves into the sand.

Suspension feeding bivalves such as common cockles have short fused siphons which maintain continuous inhalant and exhalant water currents. They obtain nutrients from plankton and detritus carried in the overlying water. Deposit-feeding molluscs such as the common otter shell often have large flexible extensible siphons which vacuum food particles from the sand surface.

## Variegated scallop

*Chlamys varia*

**Size:** up to 6 cm long
**Colour:** varies from yellow, orange to purple or brown often with patches of other colours
**Zone:** lower shore
**Habitat:** on rocks and in seaweed holdfasts
**Distribution:** widespread
**Field notes:** The variegated scallop has an oval shaped shell with lines and ridges and is attached by a byssus.

## Saddle oyster
*Anomia ephippium*

**Size:** up to 6 cm diameter
**Colour:** white to pale-brown with a blue or pink tinge
**Zone:** lower shore
**Habitat:** attached under rocks, on other shells, and on kelp holdfasts and fronds
**Distribution:** widespread
**Field notes:** The saddle oyster attaches to rocks by byssus threads though a hole in the right valve. The shell valves are unequal and very thin and brittle.

## Native, Common or Flat oyster
*Ostrea edulis*

**Size:** up to 10 cm diameter
**Colour:** off-white or cream with light brown bands
**Zone:** lower shore
**Habitat:** attached to rocks or loose on coarse sediment
**Distribution:** widely distributed around the British Isles, but less so on the east and north east coasts of Britain and Ireland.
**Field notes:** The native oyster is included in a **Species Action Plan** under the **UK Biodiversity Action Plan**.

## Common or Blue mussel
*Mytilus edulis*

**Size:** variable but can be up to 10 cm long
**Colour:** dark brown, blue-black or purple
**Zone:** middle to lower shore
**Habitat:** on rocks and boulders, in crevices and often forming large beds up to 6 layers thick
**Distribution:** widespread
**Field notes:** The common mussel shell is teardrop shaped, smooth with concentric lines, and attached to rocks by byssus threads.

## Common cockle

*Cerastoderma edule*

**Size:** up 5 cm long
**Colour:** cream to light yellow
**Zone:** middle to lower shore
**Habitat:** burrows in all types of sandy shores
**Distribution:** widespread
**Field notes:** Cockles burrow up to 5 cm in sand using a muscular foot. The shell is thick and oval with 22 – 28 radiating ribs, ridges and occasionally short spines.

The common cockle is a suspension feeder, feeding on tiny zooplankton. They feed when covered by water by opening their shells and extending a pair of short siphons. Water is drawn through one siphon, filtered, and waste products are ejected through the other siphon. It can live for 5 –10 years. Common cockles are fished commercially in many estuaries and preyed on by wading birds such as oystercatchers, and the necklace shell.

## Banded venus

*Clausinella fasciata*

**Size**: up to 2.5 cm long
**Colour:** variable, often rusty brown with darker radiating bands
**Zone:** lower shore
**Habitat:** burrows in coarse gravels with sand or shell fragments
**Distribution:** widespread
**Field notes:** The shells of the banded venus form an imperfect triangle shape. It is a shallow burrower.

## A bivalve mollusc

*Abra alba*

**Size:** up to 2.5 cm long
**Colour:** white
**Zone:** lower shore
**Habitat:** burrows in fine muddy sand
**Distribution:** widespread
**Field notes:** The small, glossy shell is oval, thin and brittle. This bivalve can feed by filtering tiny particles from the water, or by sucking up sediment with a siphon and extracting food from it. It usually lives for only one year.

## Striped venus clam

*Chamelea striatula*

**Size**: up to 4 cm long
**Colour:** dull white/cream with 3 reddish brown radiating bands
**Zone:** lower shore
**Habitat:** buried in fine to coarse sands and muddy sand
**Distribution:** widespread except for south east England
**Field notes:** The shell of the striped venus clam is thick and triangular shaped with fine ridges. It can live for around 10 years.

## Thin tellin
*Tellina tenuis*

**Size:** up to 3 cm long
**Colour:** white, rose-pink or orange shell
**Zone:** middle to lower shore
**Habitat:** buried 5-12 cms deep in fine to medium sand
**Distribution:** widespread
**Field notes:** The shiny shell is thin and brittle and triangular in shape. It is a deposit-feeder, extending a long siphon above the sand. Young flatfish often eat parts of the siphon, which can be re-grown.

3

## Common otter shell
*Lutraria lutraria*

**Size:** up to 13 cm long
**Colour:** dull white or yellowish tinted pink or purple
**Zone:** lower shore
**Habitat:** buried in sand and muddy sands
**Distribution:** widespread
**Field notes:** The common otter shell is also called a gaper and lives in a deep burrow to around 40 cm. Long siphons maintain contact with the surface of the sand, enabling it to filter feed from depth. The shell surface has fine concentric ridges and rings.

## Pod razor shell

*Ensis siliqua*

**Size:** up to 20 cm long
**Colour:** white with pink/red streaks
**Zone:** lower shore
**Habitat:** burrows in fine sand **(1)**
**Distribution:** widespread
**Field notes:** The pod razor shell lives in a deep vertical burrow. The pair of short siphons **(2)** make a key-hole shape on the surface of the sand, indicating the animal below. The long, fragile shells are straight-edged. Razor shells burrow using a strong muscular foot **(3)**. The pod razor may live for 10 – 20 years. It is an active suspension feeder, consuming organic detritus.

### DID YOU KNOW?

A buried razor shell can detect the pressure and vibration from your footsteps. If disturbed, it will retreat rapidly into its burrow and you may see a jet of water shoot into the air from the sand surface as it takes this avoiding action. On your next safari, look out for this behaviour!

## Rayed artemis

*Dosinia exoleta*

**Size:** to 6 cm diameter
**Colour:** variable with pinkish brown rays or blotches on pale background
**Zone:** lower shore
**Habitat:** burrows in muddy, coarse sand and gravel
**Distribution:** all British and Irish coasts, absent from south east England
**Field notes:** The rayed artemis has an almost circular shell marked with fine ridges.

## Pullet carpet shell

*Venerupsis senegalensis*

**Size:** up to 5 cm long
**Colour:** brownish with darker markings
**Zone:** lower shore
**Habitat:** burrows in coarse muddy sand up to 5 cm deep
**Distribution:** widespread
**Field notes:** The pullet carpet shell has lines across the shell and radiating from the top. It may be attached by a byssus to a stone buried in the sand. It feeds by filtering plankton.

## Rayed trough shell

*Mactra stultorum*

**Size:** up to 5 cm long
**Colour:** white to light purple with radiating light brown rays
**Zone:** lower shore
**Habitat:** burrows in fine to medium clean sand
**Distribution:** widespread in Britain, mainly north and north east coasts of Ireland
**Field notes:** The rayed trough shell lives in a shallow burrow and is a suspension feeder, feeding on **phytoplankton**. The shell is brittle and glossy. The strong muscular foot, used for burrowing can be seen in the image above.

## Faroe sunset shell

*Gari fervensis*

**Size:** up to 5 cm long
**Colour:** variable
**Zone:** lower shore
**Habitat:** burrows in fine sand or shell gravel
**Distribution:** widespread
**Field notes:** The Faroe sunset shell is crossed by concentric ridges and radiating rays. One end of the shell is abruptly squared off.

## Banded wedge shell

*Donax vittatus*

**Size:** up to 3.8 cm long
**Colour:** shiny white to yellow or light brown
**Zone:** middle to lower shore
**Habitat:** burrows in fine to coarse sand on moderately exposed beaches
**Distribution:** widespread
**Field notes:** The shell edge is wavy or **crenulate** with fine ridges and grooves. Bands of colour often run across the shell. The banded wedge shell lives just below the surface and is shown above next to its burrow. The background image shows the surface signs of a large group of banded wedge shells on the shore.

6. Animal life

# Bryozoans or sea mats

**Bryozoan means 'moss animal' but they are usually called sea mats. Sea mats commonly form thin encrusting patches, mainly on rocks and seaweeds. These patches are made up of a few to millions of tiny animals called zooids living together in a colony.**

Each animal lives in its own minute 'rectangular' compartment. This gives many bryozoans a fine, lacy or mesh-like appearance. In water, the **zooids** extend a ring of feeding tentacles, covered with hairs, into the current and filter out their food, which is mainly microscopic plankton.

Sea slugs feed on the zooids. Using a hand lens or magnifying glass, you can observe in close-up the structure of a bryozoan (see below). They are very difficult to identify so only two examples are included. Fossil records show bryozoans existed at least 600 million years ago.

## Hairy sea mat

*Electra pilosa*

**Size:** variable, but colonies can cover large areas. Zooids are up to 0.5 mm long.
**Colour:** silver-grey
**Zone:** middle to lower shore
**Habitat:** grows on seaweeds including serrated wrack, Irish moss and false Irish moss or on rocks
**Distribution:** widespread
**Field notes:** The hairy sea mat forms flat sheets. It appears bristly or hairy as the zooids are bordered by spines.

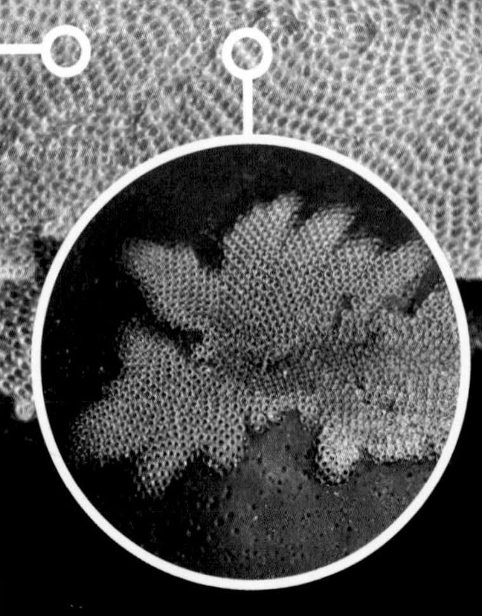

## CREATURE FEATURES

- Sea mats or 'moss animals' live in groups called colonies
- Many different growth forms
- Around 30 intertidal species
- Sessile
- Each animal is called a zooid
- They have tentacles but no stinging cells
- Mesh-like or lacy appearance
- Filter feeders
- Hermaphrodite

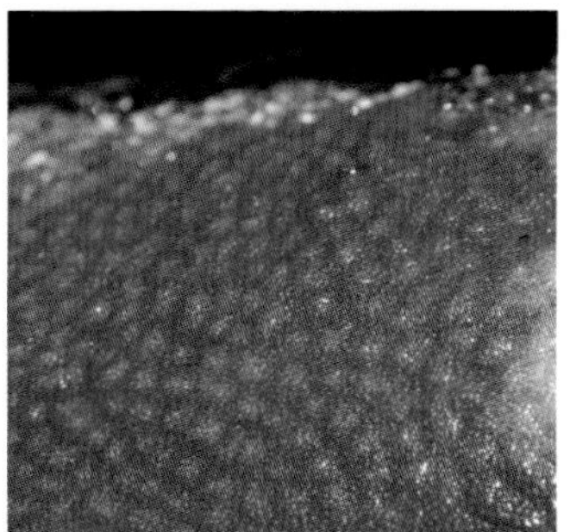

### Orange peel bryozoan

*Turbicellepora magnicostata*

**Size:** variable
**Colour:** deep orange
**Zone:** lower shore
**Habitat:** on and under boulders and on algae
**Distribution:** a southern species only found on the Isles of Scilly
**Field notes:** The orange peel bryozoan forms domed or cylindrical colonies which encrust boulders and brown seaweeds. This species is normally found in the Mediterranean.

### A bryozoan

*Flustrellidra hispida*

**Size:** each animal about 1 mm across, but colony size varies
**Colour:** purplish-brown
**Zone:** middle to lower shore
**Habitat:** grows on serrated wrack
**Distribution:** widespread
**Field notes:** This bryozoan has a gelatinous texture. The colonies are thick and bristly. Individual zooids may be visible with the naked eye. This species is predominantly found associated with algae in the intertidal zone.

# Echinoderms

**Echinoderms are 'spiny skinned' animals and those living on rocky shores include feather stars, starfish, brittlestars, sea cucumbers and sea urchins.**

The body shape can vary from being globular (sea urchins) or drawn out into five or more arms (starfish and brittlestars). **Echinoderms** have no front or back end and are based on **radial symmetry**. They are free living and most move very slowly using a series of double rows of tube feet and suckers, via a system of hydraulics.

The outer layer of the body is composed of many plates of calcium carbonate, which may link together to form a rigid 'shell' or test and spines. Echinoderms have no head and no brain. They are usually large and brightly coloured. On a sandy shore, the echinoderms are represented by several species of starfish, brittlestars and heart urchins. Their spines can help the animal burrow or bury itself in the sediment. On the west coast of the UK in particular, sea cucumbers can be found.

**Sea cucumbers** 153
**Crinoids** 154
**Starfish** 156
**Brittlestars** 160
**Sea urchins** 162

## CREATURE FEATURES

- Confined to the marine environment
- Slow moving
- Brightly coloured and very conspicuous on the seashore
- Body consists of calcareous plates closely jointed to give a rigid test, or linked by a flexible body wall
- Five-rayed (radial) symmetry
- Each of the rays consists of a narrow band of small porous plates
- They have long flexible and contractile tube feet operated by hydraulics
- Solitary animals
- Echinoderm means 'spiny skinned' and these animals have a covering of sharp spines or a rough skin

# Sea cucumbers

**Sea cucumbers belong to the class Holothuroidea.** Unlike other classes of echinoderms, sea cucumbers do not have a rigid skeleton. They have an elongate body which is soft and sausage-shaped. There are no spines present. The tube feet are usually arranged in 3 rows on the underside and 2 rows on the upper surface. In some species, these may be absent. Sea cucumbers feed on small food particles, picked up by the feeding tentacles which surround the mouth. They can be found hiding in rock crevices or buried in mud and sand. Sea cucumbers move slowly by contractions of the muscular body.

## A sea cucumber

*Leptosynapta inhaerens*

**Size:** usually 10-15 cm long but can be up to 30 cm
**Colour:** pale pink
**Zone:** lower shore
**Habitat:** burrows in muddy sand or gravel
**Distribution:** mainly south west and west coasts of Britain and Ireland and north east coast of Scotland
**Field notes:** This species of sea cucumber is worm-like, with 12 short, branching, feeding tentacles surrounding the mouth. It has soft, sticky skin and no tube feet.

## Sea gherkin

*Pawsonia saxicola*

**Size:** up to 15 cm long
**Colour:** white
**Zone:** lower shore
**Habitat:** in crevices and under boulders
**Distribution:** south and south west coasts of Britain and Ireland
**Field notes:** The sea gherkin has five distinct rows of tube feet. There are ten dark, tree-like feeding tentacles around the mouth. The cylindrical body is long, narrow and fairly smooth. The thin, flexible outer skin is strengthened with internal calcareous plates.

# Crinoids

**There are three British species which belong to the class Crinoidea, but only one, the rosy feather-star, is found in the intertidal zone of rocky shores.**

**Crinoids** have a cup-shaped body and ten flexible arms. They are a primitive group of echinoderms.

Small specimens of the rosy feather-star can be found at very low tides on the lower shore, usually on or under rocks and boulders. They are suspension feeders. Fossilised sea-lilies (around 300 million years old) are distant relatives of the rosy feather-star.

## Rosy feather-star

*Antedon bifida*

**Size:** arms 5 – 10 cm long
**Colour:** varied, often banded red/pink and white
**Zone:** lower shore on low spring tides
**Habitat:** attached to rocks and boulders, walls of gullies and on kelps or large hydroids on sheltered to moderately exposed coasts
**Distribution:** most of Britain and Ireland but absent from the southern part of the east coast of England
**Field notes:** The rosy feather-star has 10 feathery arms with 3 sizes of tube feet on each. There are no suckers on these tube feet.
On the underside, 25 short 'cirri' anchor the feather-star to rocks. It can crawl along fairly quickly. The central disc has a mouth on the upper surface. Feather-stars filter sea water and extract small food particles, passing them with their tube feet along grooves on the arms to the mouth. The background image shows 3 feather-stars under a boulder. Insert **(1)** shows a feather-star in water and **(2)** shows one hanging from the side of a boulder.

# Starfish

**Starfish belong to the Class Asteroidea and have a star-shaped body. On many rocky shores, they are the most common Echinoderms to be found. Some species live on sandy shores.**

They move using a series of extendable tube-feet under each arm **(1)**. These work by hydrostatic pressure. If you watch one moving in a rockpool, it appears to glide along. Starfish feed by gripping the two halves of mussel or oyster shells and pulling them apart, with their tube feet, which are also often equipped with suckers.

Once open, the starfish pushes or everts its stomach through the mouth **(2)**, and pours digestive juices over the body of the shellfish.

The liquid containing the dissolved shellfish is absorbed through the wall of the starfish's stomach, and the stomach is pulled back in through the mouth.

Starfish can repeatedly lose parts of arms and can regenerate new parts, provided that part of the central disc is present **(3)**.

Starfish may have between 5 and 14 arms, and when moving, any arm can take the lead. The outer body surface is often protected with short spines.

## DID YOU KNOW?

The seven armed starfish is a fierce predator. It feeds on other echinoderms especially shore urchins (p162), common brittlestars (p161) and common starfish (p157).

### Seven-armed starfish

*Luidia ciliaris*

**Size:** up to 40 cm
**Colour:** orange-brown
**Zone:** lower shore
**Habitat:** sandy or sand-scoured rocks, gravels sediments, juveniles in rockpools
**Distribution:** north, west and south west coasts of Britain and all around Irish coast
**Field notes:** This starfish has 7 arms with a band of long white spines along the sides of the arms. The seven-armed starfish can move very quickly and is the largest starfish in British waters.

### Common starfish

*Asterias rubens*

**Size:** up to 50 cm across
**Colour:** variable from orange to reddish or violet
**Zone:** middle and lower shore
**Habitat:** in rockpools, under boulders and overhangs, on rocks and on mussel beds
**Distribution:** widespread
**Field notes:** The common starfish is the most common and familiar starfish on our shores. It has a central row of white spines along each of its 5 arms. It is a carnivore with an appetite for bivalves, gastropods and crustaceans, and can often be found in large numbers feeding on mussel beds.

3

## Cushion star or Starlet

*Asterina gibbosa*

**Size:** up to 5 cm across
**Colour:** variable from dark green to pale brown, often with orange tinge
**Zone:** lower shore
**Habitat:** under boulders and overhangs, in rockpools and crevices
**Distribution:** most western and southern British and Irish coasts, except North Sea
**Field notes:** Usually has 5 short stubby arms and short orange spines on its back and around the edge of the arms. Females can lay up to 1000 orange coloured eggs on the underside of rocks and in crevices.

## A cushion star

*Asterina phylactica*

**Size:** 1.5 cm diameter
**Colour:** dark green with a darker star shape on the upper surface
**Zone:** mainly middle shore
**Habitat:** in coralline pools and under boulders of exposed shores
**Distribution:** west Wales, north and west Ireland, south west England and south west Scotland
**Field notes:** A tiny cushion star which may be confused with *Asterina gibbosa* but the dark star pattern is a key feature. The eggs are brooded and hatch as minute young cushion stars. It lives up to 4 years and the species was first described in 1979.

## Spiny starfish

*Marthasterias glacialis*

**Size:** up to 70 cm diameter
**Colour:** variable but usually grey-blue on shore
**Zone:** lower shore
**Habitat:** under rocks and boulders or in crevices and in rockpools
**Distribution:** northern and western Britain and around Ireland
**Field notes:** The spiny starfish has 3 rows of thick pointed spines along its 5 arms. Each spine is ringed with tiny 'pincers' called **pedicellariae**, which the spiny starfish uses to clean itself. The spines are usually white with purple tips. It feeds on shellfish and the common starfish.

### DID YOU KNOW?

The cushion star, lives for approximately 8 years and begins life male, changing to female at around four years old.

## 6. Animal life | Echinoderms

# Brittlestars

**Brittlestars belong to the Class Ophiuroidea. The arms of brittlestars are long and slender and very fragile. They break off easily, and so should be handled with great care.**

The arms radiate from a small central disc, and are often decorated with prominent spines. The surface of the disc may be covered with plates or scales. At the base of each arm is a pair of plates called the radial shields. There is one pair of tube feet for each joint of the arm, but they have no suckers. The tube feet are mainly used in feeding. Brittlestars can pull themselves along fairly quickly, using their arms. The mouth is rimmed with five jaws and on the underside. The colour of brittlestars can be very variable. They can be found on both rocky and sandy shores.

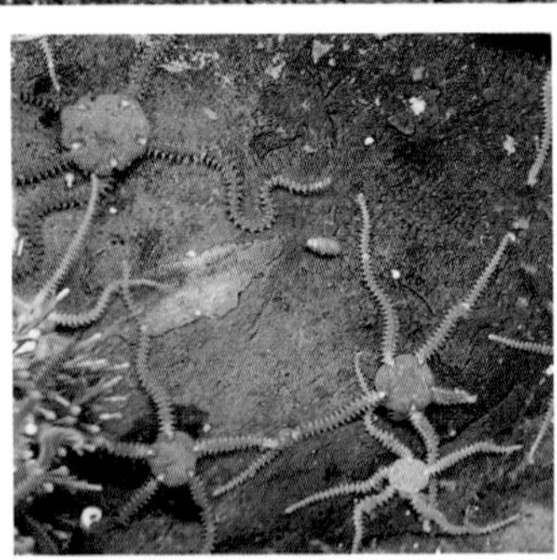

### Little Brittle star

*Amphipholis squamata*

**Size:** disc diameter 5 mm, arms up to 2 cm long
**Colour:** greyish
**Zone:** middle to lower shore
**Habitat:** amongst algal holdfasts, under rocks and boulders
**Distribution:** widespread
**Field notes:** As its common name suggests, the little brittle star is a tiny species with very thin, short arms. The central disc is circular and covered with scales. This animal is a suspension feeder, trapping detritus in mucus.

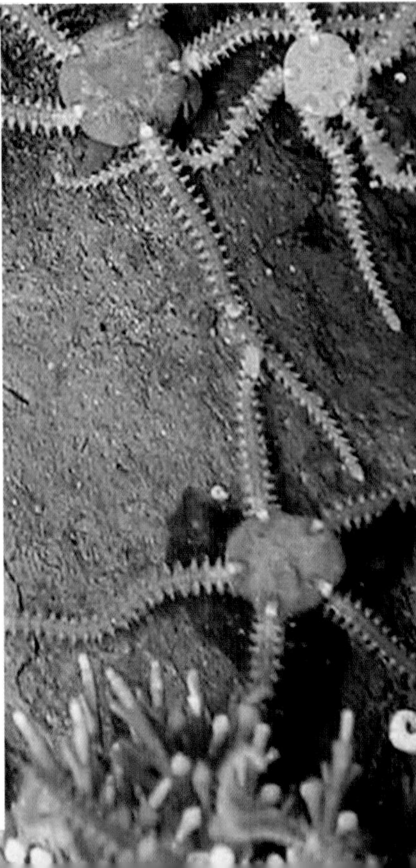

## Common Brittlestar

*Ophiothrix fragilis*

**Size:** disc up to 2 cm diameter
**Colour:** very variable, arms usually banded
**Zone:** lower shore
**Habitat:** under rocks and boulders or under algae in rockpools with suitable sandy/shell sediments
**Distribution:** widespread
**Field notes:** The common brittlestar is large, with 5 flexible, spiny arms. The central disc is pentagonal-shaped and also has spines.

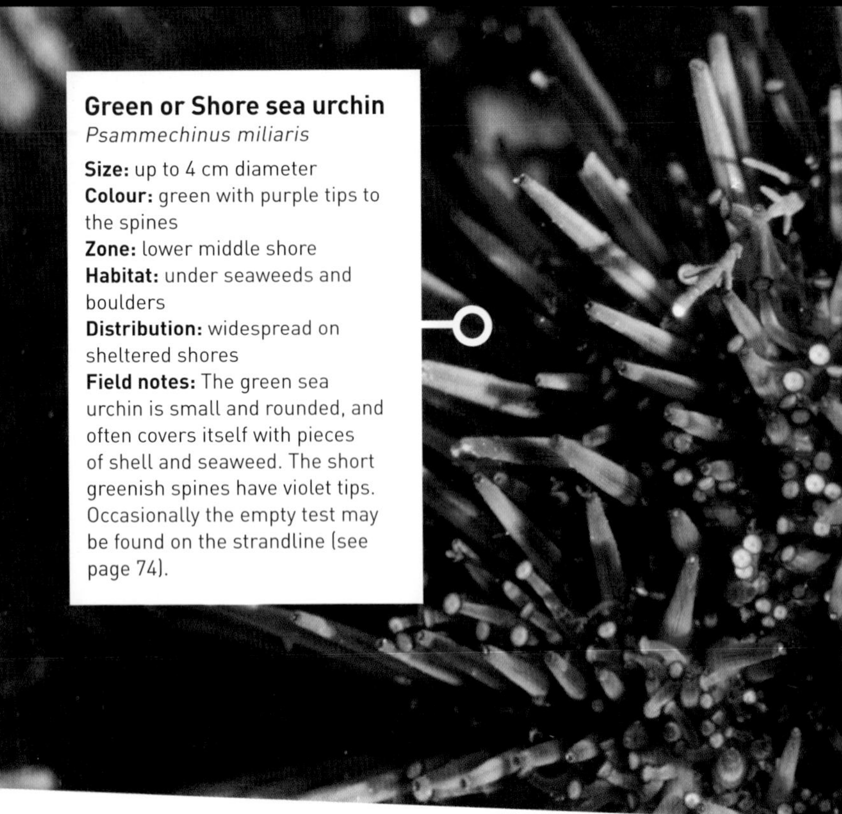

**Green or Shore sea urchin**
*Psammechinus miliaris*

**Size:** up to 4 cm diameter
**Colour:** green with purple tips to the spines
**Zone:** lower middle shore
**Habitat:** under seaweeds and boulders
**Distribution:** widespread on sheltered shores
**Field notes:** The green sea urchin is small and rounded, and often covers itself with pieces of shell and seaweed. The short greenish spines have violet tips. Occasionally the empty test may be found on the strandline (see page 74).

## 6. Animal life | Echinoderms

# Sea urchins

**Sea urchins belong to the Class Echinoidea, and many fossils exist of extinct groups of Echinoids. They have a rounded, rigid, spiny shell or test, composed of many plates.**

The test protects the soft body of the animal inside. Sea urchins move using a series of tube feet, with suckers which are found between the spines. The mouth is located underneath the animal, and it has five sharp teeth which are used to scrape small seaweeds off rocks, or to crunch barnacles and tube worms **(1)**. As they feed on plants and animals, they are called **omnivores** (see page 24). On a rocky shore, only the shore sea urchin is regularly found, but you may be lucky enough to discover a common sea urchin in lower shore pools. On the west coast of Ireland, the black sea urchin (*Paracentrotus lividus*) can also be found in large numbers, living in rock cavities. Heart urchins, such as the sea potato, live buried in sand (see page 165).

## Common or Edible sea urchin

*Echinus esculentus*

**Size:** up to 17 cm across
**Colour:** reddish/pink with purple spine tips
**Zone:** extreme lower shore and sub-littoral fringe
**Habitat:** on rocks and amongst kelp seaweeds
**Distribution:** widespread around most of Britain and Ireland
**Field notes:** This large urchin is covered in spines and tube feet. The spines are relatively short. It grazes on algae, especially kelps, and animals such as sea mats and sea firs, using a powerful tooth apparatus called the Aristotle's lantern. It may live for over 10 years.

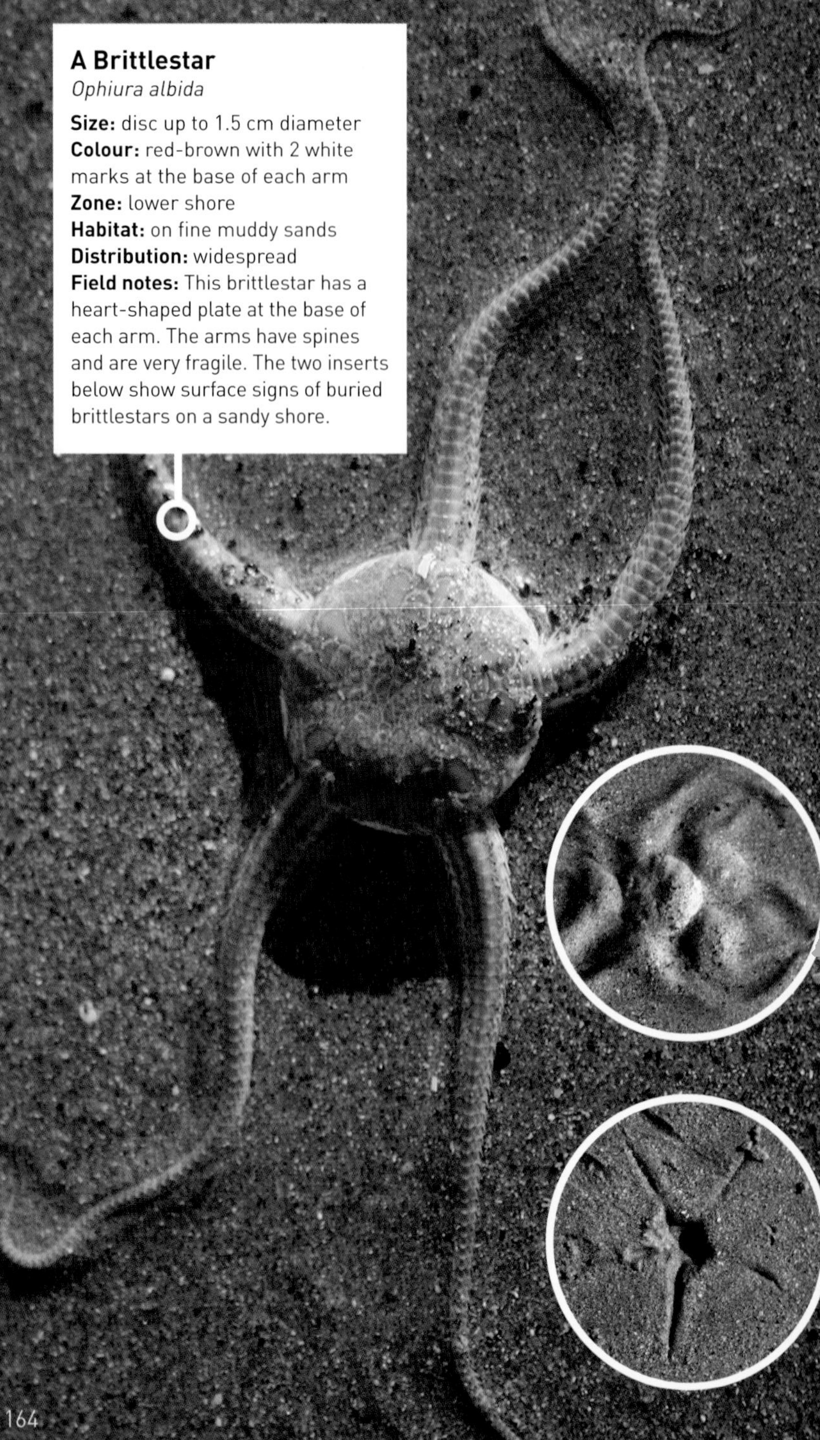

## A Brittlestar

*Ophiura albida*

**Size:** disc up to 1.5 cm diameter
**Colour:** red-brown with 2 white marks at the base of each arm
**Zone:** lower shore
**Habitat:** on fine muddy sands
**Distribution:** widespread
**Field notes:** This brittlestar has a heart-shaped plate at the base of each arm. The arms have spines and are very fragile. The two inserts below show surface signs of buried brittlestars on a sandy shore.

## A Brittlestar

*Ophiura ophiura*

**Size:** disc up to 3.5 cm diameter
**Colour:** dull grey-brown to sandy-orange
**Zone:** lower shore
**Habitat:** fine to coarse muddy sand and gravel
**Distribution:** widespread
**Field notes:** A large brittlestar with short straight arms. The disc is covered with coarse scales. It is a suspension feeder.

## Sand star

*Astropecten irregularis*

**Size:** usually 10 cm diameter but can be up to 20 cm
**Colour:** yellowish brown to pale violet
**Zone:** lower shore
**Habitat:** partly buried in top layer of fine to medium grade clean sand or sandy mud
**Distribution:** widespread
**Field notes:** The sand star is a rigid animal with a flattened body and long pointed spines edging the arms. It is well adapted for burrowing. The sand star is a predator and feeds on bivalves, worms, brittlestars and crustaceans.

## Heart urchin or sea potato

*Echinocardium cordatum*

**Size:** up to 9 cm long
**Colour:** light brown with bright yellow spines
**Zone:** lower shore
**Habitat:** deeply burrowed in a permanent burrow in fine to medium grade clean and muddy sand
**Distribution:** sheltered beaches on all British and Irish coasts
**Field notes:** A conical depression at the surface may indicate the position of the animal below, buried at a depth of 8 –15 cm. It uses its spines to burrow in the sand. The empty test may be found along the strandline (page 74).

## 6. Animal life

# Tunicates and vertebrates

**The tunicates and vertebrates are members of the Phylum Chordata – animals that, at some life stage, have a notochord (rod-like skeletal structure), a hollow dorsal nerve cord and gill slits.**

However, tunicates (Urochordata) are invertebrates and lack the well-developed backbone and skeleton found in vertebrates (Vertebrata). A vertebrate skeleton can be made of bone or cartilage, and the brain is encased in a skull.

This guide features the two main groups of chordates found on the shore – the tunicates or sea squirts and bony fish.

Only the larval stage of the sea squirt has a type of simple notochord or backbone. The bony fish, however, have a well developed internal skeleton for support, a head, tail and mostly paired fins. Fish are the most familiar **vertebrates** of rocky and sandy shores.


**Sea squirts** 168

**Fish** 172

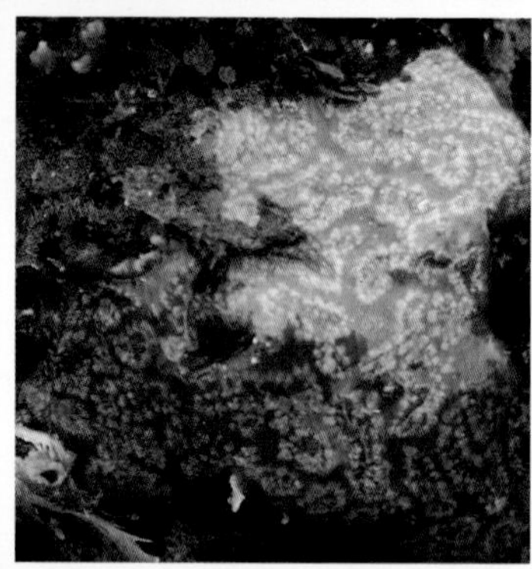

### A colonial sea squirt
*Botrylloides leachi*

**Size:** variable
**Colour:** grey, orange or red
**Zone:** lower shore
**Habitat:** encrusting rocks and shells, and on algae especially kelps
**Distribution:** widespread
**Field notes:** In this colonial sea squirt, the zooids are arranged in two parallel chains and form thick, gelatinous sheets.

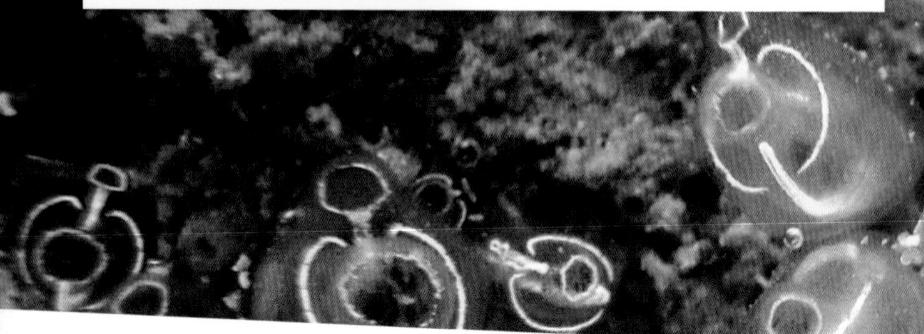

## 6. Animal life | Turnicates and vertebrates

# Sea squirts

**Sea squirts are also called tunicates or ascidians. When disturbed, they often shoot out jets of water. Ascidians are sessile and most live permanently attached to rocks or seaweeds on rocky shores.**

They belong to a special group called the **Urochordates** as the larval stage has a primitive backbone called a **notochord**. The body is contained in a tough, often transparent, outer skin or tunic. Sea squirts may occur singularly (solitary) or form jelly-like colonies of many tiny animals joined together (compound). Each solitary sea squirt has two siphons. One is an entrance and one an exit for water. Colonial sea squirts such as the star ascidian (see page 170) each have an entrance siphon, but they share an exit in the centre of each group. Each individual is called a zooid. Sea squirts filter feed, extracting tiny food particles from the water using a mucus sieve. There are many examples of non-native sea squirts on our shores such as the leathery sea squirt (page 207).

## A colonial sea squirt

*Morchellium argus*

**Size:** up to 4 cm long
**Colour:** pale orange-red or pink
**Zone:** lower shore
**Habitat:** under boulders and overhangs
**Distribution:** mostly west and south west coasts of British Isles, and scattered locations in Ireland
**Field notes:** A colonial ascidian, found in clumps hanging down in soft lobes from rocks. Each lobe consists of many zooids and has a sand covered stalk attaching it to rock. It is a suspension feeder.

## Baked bean or Gooseberry sea squirt

*Dendrodoa grossularia*

**Size:** up to 2 cm long and 1.5 cm diameter
**Colour:** reddish-brown
**Zone:** lower shore
**Habitat:** on rocks and boulders, under overhangs, in surge gullies and on large kelp holdfasts
**Distribution:** widespread
**Field notes:** The baked bean sea squirt is a solitary ascidian, often occurring in large groups. It has 2 short siphons, and can be found in both exposed and sheltered areas.

## Light bulb sea squirt

*Clavelina lepadiformis*

**Size:** up to 2 cm high
**Colour:** transparent with white outline
**Zone:** middle shore downwards
**Habitat:** attached to rocks, overhangs and large algae
**Distribution:** most coasts of Britain and Ireland
**Field notes:** The light bulb sea squirt is a colonial ascidian and forms clumps of 20 or more individuals, linked at the base. It is a suspension feeder and feeds on plankton.

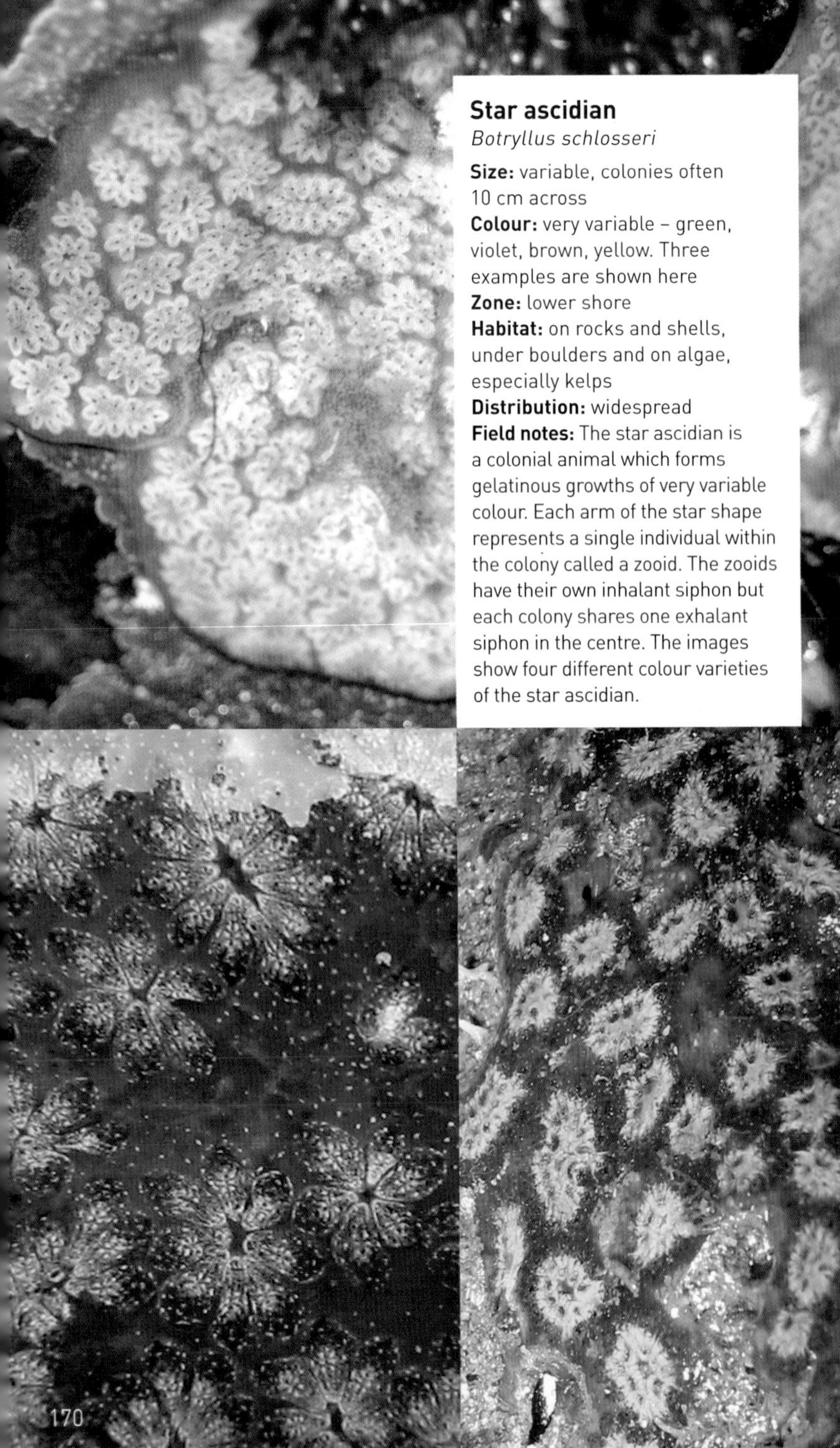

## Star ascidian

*Botryllus schlosseri*

**Size:** variable, colonies often 10 cm across
**Colour:** very variable – green, violet, brown, yellow. Three examples are shown here
**Zone:** lower shore
**Habitat:** on rocks and shells, under boulders and on algae, especially kelps
**Distribution:** widespread
**Field notes:** The star ascidian is a colonial animal which forms gelatinous growths of very variable colour. Each arm of the star shape represents a single individual within the colony called a zooid. The zooids have their own inhalant siphon but each colony shares one exhalant siphon in the centre. The images show four different colour varieties of the star ascidian.

**DID YOU KNOW?**

Both the spotted cowrie and Arctic cowrie (p.125) feed on sea squirts such as the star ascidian. They also make holes in the star ascidian colony, in which they lay their eggs.

# Fish

**The bony fish or Osteichthyes have a skeleton composed of bone and are the most advanced animals covered by this guide.**

They are all cold-blooded. They can be many shapes and colours. Seashore fish are often well-camouflaged and may be difficult to spot. Bony fish have fins for swimming, but the number and shape varies with the species. Scales usually cover the body, but some fish have a protective slimy layer instead.

They breathe using gills which extract oxygen from the water. Many of the fish found on the shore are small, and live in various micro-habitats including rockpools, under boulders or amongst seaweeds. They may also live offshore and become stranded on the shore by the outgoing tide.

Rocky shore fish are well adapted, and may have suckers (e.g. clingfish), flattened or eel-like bodies (e.g. pipefish), spines or camouflage (e.g. long-spined sea scorpion) to enable them to survive the harsh conditions.

The dominant fish species living on sandy shores are flatfish (e.g. dover sole and dab). These are important predators, feeding on worms and bivalves. Sand eels can also be found, and are an important food source for many waders and sea birds. Some fish invade sandy beaches at high tide to prey on small crustaceans, molluscs and polychaetes.

## Fifteen-spined or sea stickleback

*Spinachia spinachia*

**Size:** up to 25 cm long

**Colour:** brownish or greenish
**Zone:** lower shore
**Habitat:** amongst seaweeds and eelgrass or on sand and mud and in estuaries
**Distribution:** widespread
**Field notes:** The fifteen-spined stickleback has a tapering snout and a tiny mouth. A brown stripe runs from the snout through the eye. The body is long and thin with 14 to 17 short spines along the back. The tail fin is small and fan-shaped. This fish is well-camouflaged.

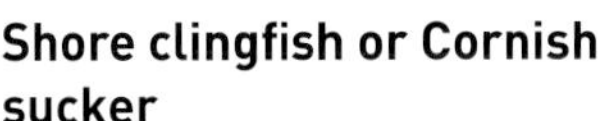

## Shore clingfish or Cornish sucker

*Lepadogaster lepadogaster*

**Size:** Up to 8 cm long
**Colour:** reddish with brown markings, and a pair of bright blue spots circled with dark brown behind each eye
**Zone:** lower shore
**Habitat:** found clinging to the underside of small boulders, crevices or in rockpools
**Distribution:** south west England, Wales, south west Scotland and Ireland
**Field notes:** The shore clingfish has no scales and a 'duck-billed' appearance. A powerful sucker disc on the underside enables it to cling to rocks (see image opposite). It has only one dorsal fin and anal fin, both attached to the tail fin. In front of each nostril is a large tentacle. The eggs can be found attached to the underside of boulders.

### CREATURE FEATURES

- Body usually covered with overlapping scales or a layer of slime
- Mouth usually at front of head
- Sexes usually separate
- Internal skeleton and backbone

## Corkwing wrasse

*Crenilabrus melops*

**Size:** up to 20 cm long
**Colour:** Males are reddish brown with bluish lines on the lower part of the head. Females are pale brown with dark brown lines on the head. Young corkwing are usually olive-green or blue-green.
**Zone:** lower shore
**Habitat:** in seaweed filled rockpools
**Distribution:** widespread, most frequent in the south and west of Britain
**Field notes:** The corkwing wrasse has a dark spot at the base of the tail. In spring, brightly coloured males build a nest from seaweed. After the female lays eggs there, the male guards them until they hatch. Corkwing wrasse may live for up to 9 years.

## Snake pipefish

*Entelerus aequoreus*

**Size:** up to 60 cm long
**Colour:** orange-brown, body rings marked by pale blue/silvery band
**Zone:** lower shore
**Habitat:** in rockpools and amongst seaweeds
**Distribution:** widespread
**Field notes:** The snake pipefish is our largest pipefish. It has a long, smooth, snake-like body. A dark reddish stripe runs through the eye, and the nose is long.

## Five-bearded rockling

*Ciliata mustela*

**Size:** up to 20 cm long
**Colour:** dark brown
**Zone:** lower shore
**Habitat:** under rocks and seaweeds and in rockpools
**Distribution:** widespread around Britain and on south east coasts of Ireland
**Field notes:** The five-bearded rockling has 5 sensory barbels protruding around the mouth. It uses these when searching for food. It is a long slender fish with no scales. This species may be confused with the Shore rockling, as they are similar in colour, and also have the same habitat preferences. The shore rockling, however, has only 3 barbels.

## Long-spined sea scorpion

*Taurulus bubalis*

**Size:** up to 20 cm long
**Colour:** variable – brown to reddish, mottled green
**Zone:** lower shore
**Habitat:** in rockpools amongst algae
**Distribution:** widespread
**Field notes:** The long-spined sea scorpion has a barbel at both corners of the mouth. This fish has no scales, but bony plates and a broad, bony head with a very large mouth and eyes. It is very well camouflaged in rockpools.

### DID YOU KNOW?

Pipefish are related to seahorses. The males look after the eggs and carry them on their bodies in an area called the brood patch on the abdomen.

## Butterfish

*Pholis gunnellus*

**Size:** up to 25 cm long
**Colour:** yellowish to reddish-brown with darker band, and up to 12 black spots outlined with white along base of dorsal fin
**Zone:** lower shore
**Habitat:** under rocks, in crevices, amongst seaweeds and in rockpools
**Distribution:** widespread
**Field notes:** The butterfish has a very slippery eel-like body and is difficult to handle. It is covered with mucus and may live up to 10 years.

## Worm pipefish

*Nerophis lumbriciformis*

**Size:** up to 15 cm long
**Colour:** dark brown, tinged green
**Zone:** lower shore
**Habitat:** under rocks and boulders and amongst seaweeds
**Distribution:** south west Britain and Ireland
**Field notes:** The worm pipefish has a long, thin, smooth body. Its short snout turns upwards. It has a small dorsal fin but no other fins. It is very well camouflaged against seaweed.

## Ballan wrasse (juvenile)

*Labrus bergylta*

**Size:** around 10cm long
**Colour:** bright emerald green
**Zone:** lower shore
**Habitat:** in rockpools
**Distribution:** widespread
**Field notes:** Juvenile ballan wrasse can sometimes be found in lower shore rockpools, where there is plenty of seaweed cover. The adults live offshore, but can occasionally become stranded in deeper rockpools. Young fish a few centimetres long are the current years brood and all develop into females. Ballan wrasse can live for up to 29 years.

## Shanny or Common blenny

*Lipophrys pholis*

**Size:** up to 13 cm long
**Colour:** variable – dark brown, speckled brownish or greenish
**Zone:** middle shore
**Habitat:** under stones and boulders, in crevices and in rockpools
**Distribution:** widespread
**Field notes:** The shanny has no scales but is covered in a layer of slime. This slime protects it and it can withstand long periods out of water. It has an eel-like body flattened from side to side. There is a single long dorsal fin. Shannies may live for up to 15 years. In winter they move offshore.

## Lesser sand eel

*Ammodytes tobianus*

**Size:** up to 20 cm long
**Colour:** greenish on back, silvery white below
**Zone:** middle to lower shore
**Habitat:** buried in sand or shingle
**Distribution:** widespread
**Field notes:** The lesser sand eel is long and thin and covered in scales. It has a pointed jaw and a single, long dorsal fin. The tailfin is short and forked. It is usually buried 20 – 50 cm deep in sand during winter. Sand eels can sometimes be found alive on the sand surface, and are an important food source for sea birds such as puffins **(1)**.

1

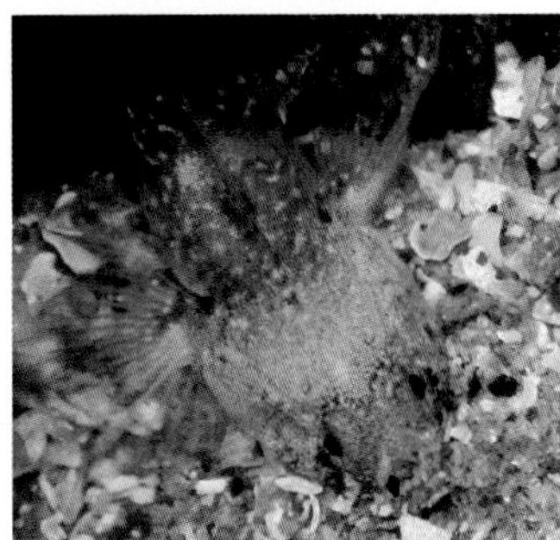

## Sand goby

*Pomatoschistus minutus*

**Size:** up to 11 cm long
**Colour:** pale brown or grey with darker markings on the sides.
**Zone:** middle to lower shore
**Habitat:** in pools on clean and muddy sand
**Distribution:** widespread
**Field notes:** The sand goby is a small fish with a slender body and a large head, which is about a quarter of the total length. The sand goby feeds on small tube worms and shrimps. The female usually lays 1-10,000 eggs under empty bivalve shells, and the male guards them. It can tolerate a wide range of temperatures and salinities and lives for 1-2 years. The sand goby is very well camouflaged in sandy pools.

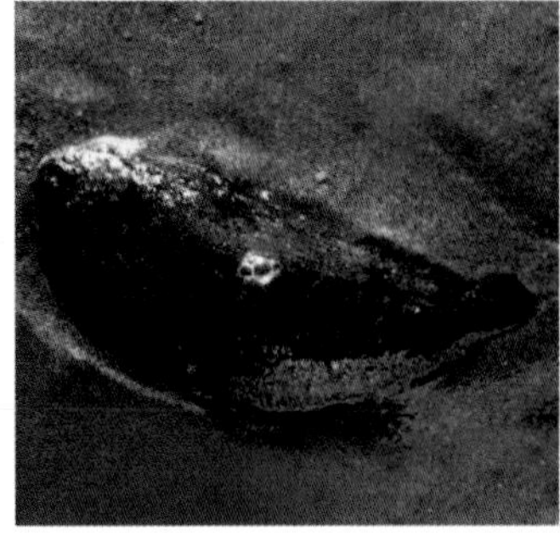

## Sole, Common sole or Dover sole

*Solea solea*

**Size:** up to 50 cm long
**Colour:** variable – grey, reddish brown or brown with irregular dark blotches
**Zone:** lower shore
**Habitat:** on sandy and muddy sediments and in pools
**Distribution:** widespread
**Field notes:** Soles are very well camouflaged and can change their colour to suit the background sediment. During the day they lie buried in sand with just their eyes poking out, or half-buried in sandy pools. They feed at night mainly on polychaetes and small bivalve molluscs. Juveniles often live on the shore. The sole is a type of flatfish with eyes and nose on the right hand side of the head. This species is included in the UK Biodiversity Action Plan for Commercial Marine Fish, but it is vulnerable to over-fishing.

# Who laid these eggs?

**It is probable that during forays along the rocky shore, you may discover many types of egg, particularly in the spring.**

Eggs may be found as large groups of capsules, embedded in protective jelly, as long strings, attached to the animal, or as an individual egg case. This is a basic guide to the more common types of egg that you may encounter.

## EGG QUIZ

Using the information found throughout the book, try and match the type of eggs shown here to the type of animal that laid them. Answers on the following pages.

1
2
3
4
5
6
7
8
9
10
11
12

# Who laid these eggs? Answers

1. **Shore crab eggs** – up to 185,000 eggs are laid, attached to the female's **pleopods**. They are orange-coloured and remain here for several months before hatching as planktonic larvae.

2. **Clingfish eggs** are laid under rocks and boulders.

3. **Common whelk eggs** are laid on rocks and on the sides of boulders, or on artificial structures like pier legs. A mass of up to 2000 egg capsules is laid. Each capsule contains up to 1000 eggs. Most do not survive. The empty egg capsules are often washed up on the strandline.

4.The **small-spotted catshark** lays an egg-case, often called a mermaid's purse. You can just see the developing embryo inside. The egg-case is up to 40 mm long with long curly tendrils at each end which attach it to seaweed. The baby catshark hatches after 8-9 months.

5. **Grey sea slug eggs** are laid under and on rocks and boulders. The spawn is a spiral thread coiled back and fore in a large mass. There may be up to 20 million eggs.

6. **Sea hare eggs** are laid on seaweeds and rocks. These pink strands may contain up to 26 million eggs.

7. **Sea lemon eggs** are laid under and on rocks and boulders. The spawn is a broad ribbon laid in a spiral attached by one edge, forming a rosette shape. Individual egg capsules are embedded in transparent jelly.

8. **Shanny eggs** are laid under rocks and boulders. You may also find the male fish guarding the eggs for around a month before they hatch. He can be seen fanning a current of water over the eggs with his fins, to keep them oxygenated.

9. **The Greenleaf worm egg** is a bright green, pear-shaped and jelly-like capsule found attached under overhangs and on seaweeds.

10. **The Netted dog whelk** lays rows of flattened, vase-shaped capsules containing tiny, yellowish eggs. These are attached to seaweeds and under overhangs.

11. Up to 150 eggs are attached to an area under the body of the male **worm pipefish**, called the brood patch, by the female. The male looks after the eggs until they hatch.

12. **Dog whelks** lay 100-1000 yellowish, flask-shaped egg capsules under rocks and boulders, and especially under overhangs.

1 Shore crab

2 Clingfish

3 Common whelk

4 Catshark

5 Grey sea slug

6 Sea hare

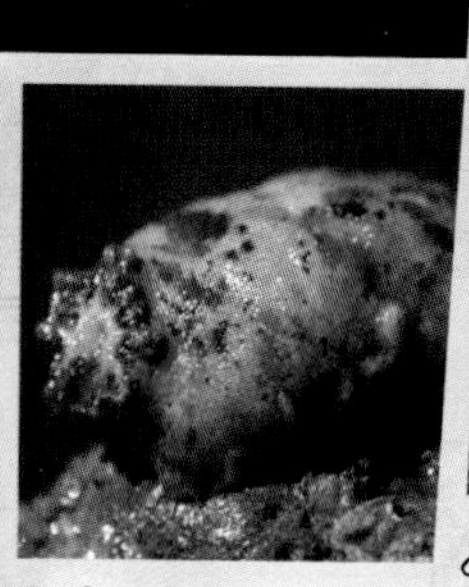
7 Sea lemon

8 Shanny

9 Green leaf worm

10 Netted dog whelk

11 Worm pipefish

12 Dog whelk

# 7. Seaweeds

**The rocky shores of Britain and Ireland are edged with a particular type of vegetation extending from the upper shore into the sub-littoral zone. This vegetation is termed marine algae, and is commonly known as seaweed.**

**Seaweeds** are not classified as plants, as they do not have true roots, stems or leaves. They also absorb nutrients needed for growth directly from the water. Most have a **holdfast** (page 186) which anchors them to rocks. This may be a small disc, or a complex structure of interwoven 'roots' called the **haptera**. The **frond** is made up of the stem or **stipe**, and **blade** or **lamina**. Alternatively, seaweeds can be bushy with many branches. Seaweeds can be **perennial** or **annual**, and some of the larger species have bladders filled with gas to increase buoyancy. All of these features are important for identification purposes. There are 3 different classes of marine algae, categorized according to the type of pigment they contain. These are the greens, browns and reds. Each group is found on certain parts of the shore, and each has different animal species depending on it for food and shelter. There are about 625 species of green, brown and red algae combined, recorded from the intertidal and shallow subtidal waters of Britain and Ireland. Some of the more commonly found seaweed species are included here. When identifying the seaweeds on your local shore, note that the colour alone cannot be used as a key feature, as it is not always obvious.

Marine algae form the basis of food webs (see page 25) and many are also used by humans as food. They are found in health food products, in cosmetics and shampoos, and in soil fertilizer.


| | |
|---|---|
| **Zonation** | **186** |
| **Green algae** | **188** |
| **Brown algae** | **190** |
| **Red algae** | **196** |

## Oyster thief

*Colpomenia peregrina*

**Size:** 1-7 cm diameter
**Colour:** greenish olive with brown spots

**Zone:** middle to lower shore
**Habitat:** attached to rocks, shells and other seaweeds
**Distribution:** widespread
**Field notes:** The oyster thief is a non-native brown seaweed (p206). It consists of a thin walled, hollow sphere, which is dry and papery to the touch.
**Origin:** Pacific Ocean. It was introduced in 1907 from France into Cornwall and Dorset.
**Effects:** Negligible in the UK. In other countries, it grows attached to oyster shells. When the oyster thief is large enough, it has the capacity to float away with the oyster, hence its common name.

### PROJECT: SEAWEEDS

Egg or knotted wrack can live for 15 years or more. It produces one air bladder per frond per year. See if you can estimate the age of any you find on your safaris.

### DID YOU KNOW?

Ice cream often contains seaweed! Irish moss (p.196) is used to thicken it. Look for the words agar, alginate, caragheen or caragheenan on food labels or E407 to find out what other products contain seaweeds.

## 7. Seaweeds

# Zonation

The brown fucoid seaweeds in particular show their own zonation pattern from the upper to the lower shore. This is illustrated opposite. The zonation is controlled by two main factors: their capacity to withstand dessication (upper shore) and the rate at which they grow (middle to lower shore). In addition, on the lower shore, the vertical distribution of different seaweeds depends on a species ability to live in low light levels. The type of rock and amount of slope of the shore also play a part.

**Upper shore**

**1. Channelled wrack**
*Pelvetia canaliculata*

**2. Spiral wrack**
*Fucus spiralis*

**Middle shore**

**3. Bladder wrack**
*Fucus vesiculosus*

**4. Egg wrack**
*Ascophylum nodosum*

**Lower shore to sub-littoral fringe**

**5. Serrated wrack**
*Fucus serratus*

**6. Kelp species**

**DID YOU KNOW?**

As many as 200 different species have been recorded living amongst one kelp holdfast **(1)**.

1. Channelled wrack
2. Spiral wrack
3. Bladder wrack
4. Egg wrack
5. Serrated wrack
6. Kelps

## 7. Seaweeds

# Green algae

**In the green algae or Chlorophyceae, the main colour pigment is chlorophyll which absorbs the red and blue light end of the spectrum. Other light wavelengths are reflected and account for the green colour.**

Green seaweeds are found mainly higher up the shore and in shallow water where light is plentiful. There are around 100 species of green seaweeds found on the shore in Britain and Ireland.

### Sea lettuce

*Ulva lactuca*

**Size:** up to 30 cm across
**Colour:** pale to dark green
**Zone:** upper shore to lower shore
**Habitat:** attached to rocks and stones and in rockpools
**Distribution:** widespread
**Field notes:** The frond of sea lettuce is usually wider at the top than the base and is crumpled. It is translucent and membraneous and attached to rock by a small holdfast. Sea lettuce is eaten by the sea hare (see page 137).

## Gutweed

*Ulva intestinalis*

**Size:** fronds 10 – 30 cm long and 6 – 18 mm diameter
**Colour:** bright grass green
**Zone:** upper to lower shore
**Habitat:** on rocks, in rockpools
**Distribution:** widespread
**Field notes:** The fronds are long, thin inflated tubes with narrow tips. Gutweed can thrive where there is freshwater running down the shore. It is a summer annual seaweed and commonly grows on other algae and shells.

## Velvet horn

*Codium tomentosum*

**Size:** up to 30 cm long
**Colour:** dark green
**Zone:** lower shore
**Habitat:** on exposed rocks and in rockpools
**Distribution:** mainly south west Britain and scattered around the coast of Ireland and western Scotland
**Field notes:** The spongy, branching fronds of velvet horn have a soft, velvety texture with colourless hairs. The holdfast is disc shaped.

## A green seaweed

*Cladophora rupestris*

**Size:** separate threads up to 12 cm long and up to 20 cm high
**Colour:** dark green
**Zone:** mid to lower shore
**Habitat:** in rockpools, in crevices and under other seaweeds
**Distribution:** widespread
**Field notes:** Moss-like and made up of many fine threads forming dense tufts. It occurs throughout the year.

7. Seaweeds

# Brown algae

**In the brown algae or Phaeophyceae, chlorophyll is masked by a brown pigment called fucoxanthin.**

This absorbs light at the yellow part of the spectrum, so the brown seaweeds are found mainly on the middle shore and thrive in deeper water than green seaweeds. Brown seaweeds can in fact be various colours including brown, yellowish-brown and olive. Many species of brown algae have air bladders which help the blades of the algae float toward the sea surface, allowing for maximum sunlight absorption. There are around 200 species of brown algae found on the shores of Britain and Ireland.

### A brown seaweed

*Dictyota dichotoma*

**Size:** 10 – 15 cm high, fronds up to 1.2 cm wide and 7.5 – 30 cm long
**Colour:** yellowish–olive brown often with blue-green iridescence in water
**Zone:** lower shore
**Habitat:** on rocks and other seaweeds in rockpools
**Distribution:** south west Britain and south and west Ireland
**Field notes:** The fronds have no midrib and are branched with rounded or notched tips.

### Tamarisk weed, Rainbow wrack or Peacock weed

*Cystoseira tamariscifolia*

**Size:** 30 – 45 cm high, 60 cm long
**Colour:** dark brown with bright green-blue iridescence under water
**Zone:** lower shore
**Habitat:** on rocks or in rockpools
**Distribution:** a southern species found in south western Britain and western Ireland
**Field notes:** Rainbow wrack is a rough, bushy seaweed covered with short spines and with a brilliant blue colour in rockpools.

## Sea oak

*Halidrys siliquosa*

**Size:** 0.3 – 1 m long
**Colour:** golden brown
**Zone:** middle to lower shore
**Habitat:** in rockpools
**Distribution:** widespread
**Field notes:** Sea oak is a bushy seaweed with alternate branches, giving a 'zig zag' appearance. The main stem is flattened and it has gas bladders which resemble long seed pods. It is sometimes called podweed because of this. The holdfast is cone shaped. Sea oak is a **perennial** species, present on the shore all year round.

## A brown seaweed

*Bifurcaria bifurcata*

**Size:** 30 – 50 cm long, up to 50 cm high
**Colour:** olive-yellow
**Zone:** middle and lower shore, especially exposed on exposed shores
**Habitat:** on rocks in pools
**Distribution:** a southern species found on south and west coasts of England and the west coast of Ireland
**Field notes:** The frond is unbranched and cylindrical. Air bladders may be present. It is a perennial species and an indicator of climate change (page 203).

## Egg or Knotted wrack

*Ascophyllum nodosum*

**Size:** fronds 0.5 – 2 m long
**Colour:** yellowish to olive green
**Zone:** middle shore
**Habitat:** on rocks of sheltered shores
**Distribution:** widespread
**Field notes:** Egg wrack has long, narrow, strap-like fronds with large egg-shaped gas bladders. There are often clumps of a red, tufty seaweed (*Polysiphonia lanosa*) attached, commonly called 'egg wrack wool' (p.198). Egg wrack has no mid-rib and is slow growing.

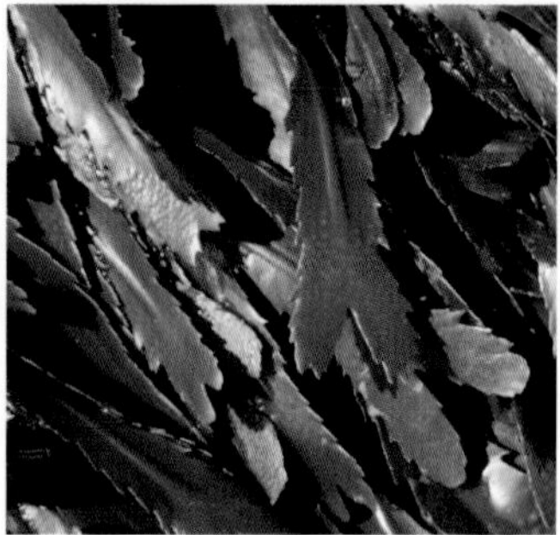

## Serrated, Saw or Toothed wrack

*Fucus serratus*

**Size:** around 60 cm long, fronds 2 cm wide
**Colour:** olive to golden brown
**Zone:** lower shore
**Habitat:** on rocks on more sheltered areas of coast
**Distribution:** widespread
**Field notes:** In serrated wrack the midrib is obvious and there are no gas bladders. The edges of the fronds are jagged, like a saw, and repeatedly split in two.

## Spiral wrack

*Fucus spiralis*

**Size:** 15 – 20 cm long
**Colour:** olive-brown
**Zone:** upper shore
**Habitat:** on rocks
**Distribution:** widespread
**Field notes:** Spiral wrack forms a band below channelled wrack on sheltered to moderately exposed shores. The midrib is prominent, and there are no gas bladders present. There are often pairs of reproductive bodies on the tips of the frond branches. The frond is often twisted.

## Channelled wrack

*Pelvetia canaliculata*

**Size:** up to 15 cm high
**Colour:** dark greenish-brown
**Zone:** upper shore
**Habitat:** on rocks
**Distribution:** widespread
**Field notes:** Channelled wrack often forms a band just above high water level of neap tides. The frond has no midrib, and there are no gas bladders present. There may, however, be swollen reproductive bodies on the tips of the fronds.

## Bladder wrack

*Fucus vesiculosus*

**Size:** up to 1 m long
**Colour:** dark olive brown
**Zone:** middle shore
**Habitat:** on rocks
**Distribution:** widespread
**Field notes:** In bladder wrack, there is a distinct midrib and pairs of rounded air bladders. The frond is branched. Bladder wrack is often found with egg wrack below spiral wrack. It lives for 4-5 years.

## Thongweed

*Himanthalia elongata*

**Size:** buttons up to 3 cm across, reproductive 'ribbons' up to 2 m long
**Colour:** olive-green
**Zone:** lower shore above Laminarians
**Habitat:** in deep rockpools or on rocks on moderately exposed shores
**Distribution:** all coasts of Britain and Ireland except south east England
**Field notes:** Thongweed can be found in two different forms. A small button or disc shaped algae can be found attached by a short stalk to rock **(1)**. These are the first year's growth. During February to May, long ribbon-like reproductive fronds **(2)** may grow out from these 'buttons'. These are the second year's growth. They eventually snap off and can often be found washed up on the strandline.

## Sugar kelp or Sea belt

*Saccharina latissima*

**Size:** up to 4 m long
**Colour:** yellowish to dark blackish brown
**Zone:** lower shore to sub-littoral
**Habitat:** in deep pools and on rocks
**Distribution:** widespread
**Field notes:** The frond is long and ruffled with wavy edges with no midrib. A small branching holdfast attaches sugar kelp to rocks. It prefers sheltered conditions and has a lifespan of 2-4 years. This seaweed is sometimes called 'Poor man's weatherglass' as it has been used traditionally to forecast the weather. If it dries up, the weather will be fine. If it swells up and becomes damp, rain is on the way.

## Oarweed or Tangle

*Laminaria digitata*

**Size:** fronds 2 m or more long
**Colour:** glossy dark brown
**Zone:** lower shore
**Habitat:** attached to bedrock
**Distribution:** most coasts of Britain and Ireland
**Field notes:** The stem is long and smooth, and out of water it bends over. Colonies of bryozoans are often found on the **blade**. The broad frond splits into 'fingers' and there is no midrib. The holdfast is dome shaped. Oarweed flourishes in moderately exposed areas.

### DID YOU KNOW?

There is a quick way of telling the difference between cuvie and oarweed. Oarweed has a smooth stipe and the frond lies flat on the shore when the tide is out. Cuvie has a rough stem, often with red seaweeds attached. It stands upright when the tide is out.

## Furbelows

*Saccorhiza polyschides*

**Size:** 4.5 m long and up to 3.5 m wide
**Colour:** golden brown
**Zone:** lower shore
**Habitat:** attached to rocks
**Distribution:** most coasts of Britain and Ireland
**Field notes:** A key identification feature is the holdfast (see above), which consists of a large, hollow bulbous structure with a warty surface. The stipe is short and flat with very wavy edges. It twists at the base. There is no midrib (see page 38).

## Cuvie

*Laminaria hyperborea*

**Size:** up to 3.5 m long
**Colour:** blade is glossy golden brown to dark brown
**Zone:** lower shore of exposed shores
**Habitat:** attached to rocks
**Distribution:** most coasts of Britain and Ireland
**Field notes:** Cuvie has a rough stem which is often covered with other seaweeds, bryozoans and hydroids growing on it. At low tide, the stem will stand upright. In sheltered areas, it may live for up to 12 years.

## Dabberlocks

*Alaria esculenta*

**Size:** 1 – 1.5 m long
**Colour:** yellowish to olive green or reddish brown
**Zone:** at low water on exposed shores
**Habitat:** attached to rocks
**Distribution:** south west England, Wales, Scotland and Ireland, also the Shetland Isles and east Scotland to Flamborough Head on the east coast of England
**Field notes:** It has a distinctive thick midrib which is a continuation of the short stem. The blade has wavy edges, which may be torn by wave action. The holdfast is claw shaped.

# Red algae

**The red algae or Rhodophyceae have red pigments called phycoerythrin and phycocyanin which mask the green chlorophyll.**

These seaweeds absorb blue light and reflect red light and so can live deeper in the sea than green or brown seaweeds. They are found mainly on the lower shore. There are around 325 intertidal species of red algae in Britain and Ireland. They can be red, pinkish-red or purple in colour.

## Irish moss or Carragheen

*Chondrus crispus*

**Size:** up to 22 cm long
**Colour:** dark purplish red, but greenish-yellow in brightly lit areas. In water, the frond tips often have a blue-purple iridescence
**Zone:** middle to lower shore
**Habitat:** on rocks and in rockpools
**Distribution:** widespread
**Field notes:** The fronds are flat and wide with rounded tips, and they divide repeatedly into two branches. The holdfast is disc shaped. Irish moss is harvested commercially as carragheen and used in the food industry.

## Pepper dulse

*Osmundea pinnatifida*

**Size:** very variable from 7-20 cm long
**Colour:** brownish-purple on lower shore, or yellowish green in brightly lit areas higher up the shore
**Zone:** middle to lower shore
**Habitat:** on rocks and in crevices on exposed to moderately sheltered shores
**Distribution:** widespread
**Field notes:** This seaweed has a distinctive 'peppery' smell. It may cover large areas forming a turf. The fronds branch alternately.

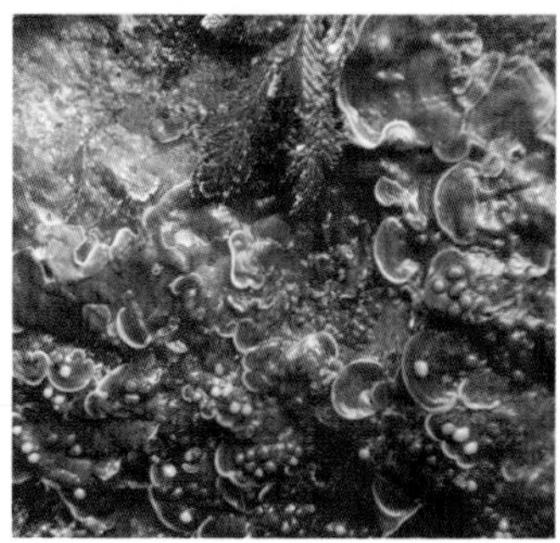

## Encrusting coralline algae

*Lithophyllum and Lithothamnion species*

**Size:** up to 20 mm thick
**Colour:** pink-purple or greyish-pink
**Zone:** lower shore
**Habitat:** on rocks, in rockpools and under algae
**Distribution:** widespread, but rare on the east coast of England between Yorkshire and east Kent
**Field notes:** These coralline algae may completely cover rocks with patches or overlapping frilly edges.

## A red seaweed

*Lomentaria articulata*

**Size:** up to 10 cm long, and up to 10 cm tall
**Colour:** shiny dark brown to bright red
**Zone:** middle to lower shore
**Habitat:** on rocks, in rockpools, under overhangs and under other algae
**Distribution:** widespread
**Field notes:** The segmented fronds look like strings of small sausages. This seaweed thrives in shady places.

## Coral weed

*Corallina officinalis*

**Size:** up to 12 cm high
**Colour:** pinkish-purple with white ends
**Zone:** middle to lower shore
**Habitat:** fringing rockpools and gullies
**Distribution:** widespread
**Field notes:** Coral weed is made up of short, rigid, calcareous segmented fronds with white tips. They often form a turf, and have a disc shaped holdfast.

## Egg wrack wool

*Polysiphonia lanosa*

**Size:** up to 70 mm long
**Colour:** brownish-red
**Zone:** middle to lower shore
**Habitat:** grows mainly on the brown seaweed egg wrack (*Ascophyllum nodosum* page192)
**Distribution:** widespread
**Field notes:** Egg wrack wool is a tufty seaweed made up of branching filaments. It looks like small 'pom poms'. It is an epiphyte, a plant that grows on other plants for physical support. In this case egg wrack wool benefits from egg wrack's buoyancy at high tide, lifting it closer to the sunlight.

## False Irish moss

*Mastocarpus stellatus*

**Size:** up to 17 cm long
**Colour:** reddish-brown to purple
**Zone:** lower shore
**Habitat:** on rocks and in rockpools in exposed areas
**Distribution:** widespread, but most abundant on western coasts
**Field notes:** This may be confused with Irish moss but in false Irish moss the edges of the ends of the fronds curl inwards to form a channel. The reproductive bodies, shown in the background image, look like small grape pips.

## Dulse

*Palmaria palmata*

**Size:** 20 – 50 cm long
**Colour:** dark red with purplish tints under water
**Zone:** lower shore
**Habitat:** on rocks and on stipes of cuvie
**Distribution:** widespread, but absent from much of eastern England
**Field notes:** The blade is membraneous with no midrib. The small holdfast is disc shaped.

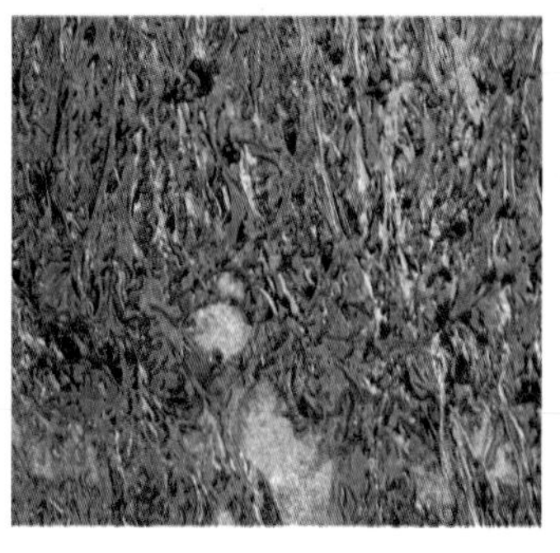

## Purple laver

*Porphyra umbilicalis*

**Size:** up to 20 cm across
**Colour:** young algae are greenish becoming purple-red when older
**Zone:** middle to lower shore
**Habitat:** attached to rock
**Distribution:** widespread
**Field notes:** The frond is thin and membraneous and irregularly shaped. It has a polythene-like texture. In south Wales, this seaweed is boiled and eaten as a delicacy called 'laverbread'.

## A red seaweed

*Catenella caespitosa*

**Size:** up to 2 cm tall
**Colour:** dark purple to nearly black
**Zone:** upper and middle shore
**Habitat:** on rock in damp shady and sheltered areas
**Distribution:** widespread
**Field notes:** Mossy group of branching fronds. May be confused with the lichen *Lichina pygmaea* (page 31), which occurs on the upper shore.

# 8. Conservation

**Our coastline and shores may have many thriving habitats and associated wildlife but also face many threats. These range from climate change to coastal development and marine litter, and some of these are outlined here. These threats are of major concern, because approximately 50% of the UK's biodiversity is found in the sea.**

There are many actions you can take at home and on the beach to help to conserve our beaches and seas. Even in small ways, you really can make a difference. By helping to ensure that intertidal habitats are protected and managed sustainably, you will help to guarantee that future generations will continue to be amazed and enticed by the wonders of the shore.

**Threats to our shores** 202
**Beach litter** 204
**Non-native species** 206
**How you can help** 210
**Where to report your findings** 212

### TOP TEN LITTER ITEMS

1. Plastic pieces under 2.5cm
2. Plastic pieces over 2.5cm
3. Crisp / sweet / lolly / sandwich wrappers
4. Plastic rope / cord / string
5. Plastic caps / lids
6. Polystyrene pieces
7. Plastic drinks bottles
8. Fishing net and net pieces under 50cm
9. Cotton bud sticks
10. Cigarette stubs

(ref: MCS Beachwatch 2009)

Promoting marine conservation

**Page 201:** 1. Become a volunteer recorder; 2. Beach litter – a threat to our marine life; 3. Snakelocks anemone – a climate change indicator; 4. Report your jellyfish sightings.

## 8. Conservation

# Threats to our shores

**Our seas and shores, including their wildlife, face many threats on a daily basis. Some of the greatest dangers include coastal erosion, coastal development, climate change, pollution and non-native species.**

**Erosion** is a natural process, whereby constant wind and wave action cuts into soft rocks, causing them to be broken down. Erosion and disturbance by increased numbers of visitors to the coast can cause habitats to change, and some sensitive species to disappear. Coastal erosion is expected to increase with climate change. Sewage, oil and industrial wastes are major pollutants, which can poison and contaminate many marine animals and plants. Rocky and sandy shores are vulnerable to all types of marine pollution. Trampling by large numbers of holidaymakers, and the collection of organisms for fishing bait by anglers, are also threats to the wildlife of rocky and sandy shores. The intertidal environment can be altered by the construction of piers, jetties, outfalls and sea defences. Intertidal biodiversity provides us with a measure of our environmental quality. Some species can help to indicate pollution and others climate change. The threats posed by climate change, marine litter and non-native species in particular are highlighted here.

**Climate change**

As the British Isles is located where creatures from the warmer Atlantic waters in the south west meet those from the colder waters of the North Sea, climate change impacts are likely to be noticeable in our intertidal habitats. Changes

Bait digging

Holidaymakers

Vehicles on the beach

have been recorded since the 1980s by marine scientists, in relation to the abundance and distribution of intertidal species. You can help marine scientists by looking for and recording climate change indicator species during your seashore safaris. Information on where to send your records is given on pages 212-213.

**Fascinating facts**

- 2006 was the second warmest year in UK coastal waters since records began in 1870.
- Since the 1980s, the rate of sea surface temperature rise has been about 0.2 to 0.6 °C per decade.
- Average seawater temperature is predicted to rise by 2°C by the 2050s.
- Southern warm water species such as flat and toothed top shells have extended their range northwards since the mid 1980s in Wales, Northern Ireland and Scotland. It is likely that this has occurred in response to climatic warming.
- As sea temperatures rise, cold water or northern species will lose out, as they retreat further northwards, leaving the British Isles.
- The sea level rise that is predicted to occur as a consequence of climate change will have a major impact on rocky shores, with the loss of entire communities of organisms.

**Climate change indicator species to search for:**

- **Shore clingfish**
- **Strawberry anemone**
- **Worm pipefish**
- **Toothed top shell**
- **Snakelocks anemone**
- **Furrowed or Montagu's crab**
- **Volcano barnacle**
- **A brown seaweed** *Bifurcaria bifurcata*

Furrowed crab

Strawberry anemone

## 8. Conservation

# Beach litter and quiz

**Litter found on our beaches is often washed ashore after being dumped or lost by ships. It is also carelessly dropped by beach visitors. Other important sources include discarded fishing nets, lines and weights by commercial and recreational fishing, fly-tipped rubbish and sewage related debris. In particular, items constructed of plastics are a great danger to many animals.**

The Marine Conservation Society annual Beachwatch Survey (2009) found that total beach litter in the UK had increased by 77% since the survey began in 1994. Plastic litter in particular was found to have increased by a staggering 121%. All of this litter can take a very long time to break down or degrade and disappear from the environment. It can also have disastrous impacts on our marine wildlife which is killed and injured by litter. Death to seabirds, dolphins and porpoises is caused by drowning from entanglement in lost or abandoned fishing net and line. Turtles accidentally swallow plastic bags and balloons, mistaking them for their favourite food of jellyfish. This litter blocks their gut and leads to their death. By becoming more aware of the impacts of our actions, we can take simple steps to ensure that our litter does not contribute to this. More information on how you can help our marine wildlife is given on pages 210-211.

**BEACH LITTER QUIZ**

Can you guess how long these man-made strandline items take to degrade and what their impacts may be on our marine wildlife?

1 Aluminium can

2 Can holder (Ringo)

3 Plastic bottle

4 Crisp packet

5 Fishing net

6 Plastic bag

7 Cotton bud stick

8 Glass

**Beach litter quiz answers:** 1 Aluminium can – 400 years; 2 Can holder – 400 years; 3 Plastic drinks bottle – 400+ years; 4 Crisp packet – 75 years; 5 Fishing net – 600 years; 6 Plastic bag – 30+ years; 7 Cotton bud stick – 450+ years; 8 Glass bottle – 1 million+ years.

## 8. Conservation

# Non-native species

**Non-native species are those which have been introduced from outside of their native geographical range or habitat. There are about 65 known established non-native marine species in Britain.**

While some non-native marine species may have arrived by natural dispersion, many have been accidentally introduced via attachment to ships or in **ballast water**. They can also arrive attached to floating litter or to other animals or plants. They are extremely difficult to eliminate once here, and may compete with our native species for space to live and food. Those with a negative impact on our shores are called **invasive species**. The impact of some non-native species may be unknown or beneficial as they could, for example, provide a new habitat. By keeping your own records of the occurrence and abundance of non-native species, and reporting this information, you can help scientists to track changes in distribution, and understand their impact on our native flora and fauna. Information on how to do this is given on page 213.

### Non-native species to record on your seashore safaris include:

1. **Wireweed** *Sargassum muticum* (p.208)
2. **Oyster thief** *Colpomenia peregrina* (p.185)
3. **Harpoon weed** *Asparogopsis armata*
4. **Wakame** *Undaria pinnatifida*
5. **A barnacle** *Austrominius modestus*
6. **Portuguese or Pacific oyster** *Crassostrea gigas* (p.209)
7. **American slipper limpet** *Crepidula fornicata* (p.208)
8. **A sea squirt** *Corella eumyota* (p.207)
9. **Leathery sea squirt** *Styela clava* (p.207)
10. **Australian tube worm** *Ficopomatus enigmaticus* (p.209)
11. **American oyster drill** *Urosapinx cinerea*
12. **Chinese mitten crab** *Eriocheir sinensis*
13. **Orange sheath tunicate** *Botrylloides violaceus* (p.207)
14. **A bryozoan** *Tricellaria inopinata* (p.209)

## Leathery sea squirt

*Styela clava*

**Size:** up to 12 cm tall
**Colour:** brown
**Zone:** lower shore
**Habitat:** attached to rocks, under boulders and overhangs
**Distribution:** south and south west England and Wales and southern Ireland
**Field notes:** The leathery sea squirt is a club-shaped solitary ascidian, attached by a tough stalk. The surface is lumpy. The two siphons on the top are close together.
**Origin:** It was introduced from Korea accidentally, attached to warships in World War II.
**Effects:** A fouling pest of marinas, moorings and boats.

## A sea squirt

*Corella eumyota*

**Size:** 2 – 4 cm diameter.
**Colour:** semi transparent with orange-pink tint to siphons
**Zone:** lower shore
**Habitat:** attached to rocks or under boulders
**Distribution:** first recorded in 2004 in the UK on the south coast, distribution not fully known
**Field notes:** This solitary sea squirt is attached to rock by its side and may be found as an individual or in clumps.
**Origin:** Southern hemisphere: South Africa, New Zealand and South America.
**Effects:** Can smother other animals and is a fouling pest of boats.

## Orange sheath tunicate

*Botrylloides violaceus*

**Size:** variable sized sheets around 2 – 3 mm thick
**Colour:** orange, yellow, red or dull purple
**Zone:** lower shore
**Habitat:** piers, boulders, marinas and docks
**Distribution:** Milford Haven (Wales) and southern England
**Field notes:** Forms firm, jelly-like flat colonies. The individual animals or zooids are large.
**Origin:** North west Pacific. It may have been introduced through ships ballast water and aquaculture.
**Effects:** It often overgrows other animals.

## American slipper limpet

*Crepidula fornicata*

**Size:** up to 2.5 cm high and 5 cm long
**Colour:** white, cream or pinkish with streaks and blotches
**Zone:** lower shore
**Habitat:** attached to stones and shells such as mussels and oysters as well as on sediment
**Distribution:** from the east coast of England and along the south coast up to Cardigan Bay in Wales
**Field notes:** It forms chains or stacks of 10 individuals or more. The shell is thick with a shelf on the underside **(1)**.
**Origin:** The slipper limpet was introduced with oysters from north east America in 1887.
**Effects:** The slipper limpet competes with the native oyster for space and food, and also threatens commercial common mussel beds. It can occur in high numbers offshore, smothering other species and altering the sea bed.

1

## Wireweed

*Sargassum muticum*

**Size:** fronds over 1 m
**Colour:** olive-brown
**Zone:** lower shore
**Habitat:** attached to rocks in rockpools
**Distribution:** south and south west England, Wales, north and south Ireland and south west Scotland
**Field notes:** Wireweed is a type of large brown seaweed. This bushy, branching seaweed has small round air bladders and flattish oval blades.
**Origin:** Introduced from the Pacific on oysters.
**Effects:** Wireweed is an invasive species which is fast growing. It competes with our native species such as seagrasses and can cover other plants and animals especially in rockpools. Image **(2)** below shows the length of wireweed. When held up, it resembles a 'washing line'.

2

## Portuguese or Pacific oyster

*Crassostrea gigas*

**Size:** up to 18 cm long
**Colour:** off-white to bluish grey with purple patches
**Zone:** lower shore
**Habitat:** attached to rocks
**Distribution:** scattered locations around Britain and Ireland
**Field notes:** The Portuguese oyster is a bivalve mollusc with very frilly, ridged shells.
**Origin:** The Pacific, then introduced to Portugal and the UK, deliberately for food.
**Effects:** It may compete for food and space with native species including the native oyster and common mussel, as it can form large beds.

## Australian tube worm

*Ficopomatus enigmaticus*

**Size:** tube 2 mm wide and up to 8 cm long
**Colour:** white tube
**Zone:** lower shore in estuaries and brackish water areas
**Habitat:** on rocks or other hard surfaces
**Distribution:** south west England, south Wales and south west Ireland
**Field notes:** It forms reefs often several layers thick. The cylindrical tubes resemble 'bamboo' and have thicker collar shaped rings along them.
**Origin:** Indian Ocean, possibly in ships ballast water or introduced with farmed oysters.
**Effects:** May displace native species.

## A bryozoan

*Tricellaria inopinata*

**Size:** up to 2 cm tall
**Colour:** light brown
**Zone:** lower shore
**Habitat:** attached to rocks and seaweeds and other surfaces in marinas and harbours
**Distribution:** south and north west England, south Wales
**Field notes:** A small bushy, branching upright bryozoan.
**Origin:** Temperate Pacific: North America, Japan to Taiwan, Australia. It may have arrived on imported oysters or attached to boats hulls.
**Effects:** Fouling of marinas and hulls of boats.

8. Conservation

# How you can help

**There are many ways in which you can help to conserve our seashores. These are some examples.**

**Take action at home**

- Don't flush cotton bud sticks or anything else you shouldn't down the toilet, including nappies and sanitary products. These often end up on the beach or in the sea, and may harm animals. In the Marine Conservation Society 2009 annual Beachwatch litter survey, cotton bud sticks were the ninth highest recorded item. Bag them and bin them instead.
- Only buy fish caught using sustainable methods not harmful to marine habitats. You can obtain a 'Good Fish Guide' from the Marine Conservation Society.
- Conserve water – turn off the tap when you clean your teeth.
- Use eco-friendly kitchen and bathroom products. Make sure that rubbish, chemicals and detergents are disposed of properly. Remember, most drains lead to the sea.
- Do not release balloons, or encourage mass balloon launches at your school or town. When they float back down, they can end up on the beach or in the sea, and harm wildlife such as dolphins, turtles and seabirds.
- Say no to plastic bags and help to save marine biodiversity. Opt for re-usable canvas bags instead. If plastic bags end up in the sea they can kill turtles, as they can mistake them for jellyfish, which are their main food.

Volunteer to carry out a strandline survey for shark and ray egg-cases

Volunteer to carry out a beach clean of your local beach

- Always cut up plastic bottle and drinks can yokes 'Ringos' before you dispose of them. Many animals have been found entangled in them.

**Take action on the beach**

- When exploring any seashore, always follow the Seashore Code shown on page 15.
- Become a volunteer recorder. Take part in the Marine Life Information Network (MarLIN) Sealife Survey, and report anything you find on the shore to the organisation.
- Use the bins provided at the beach, or take all of your litter home after visiting the beach or coast, including disposable barbecues.
- Don't buy any shells, dried seahorses, pufferfish, or sharks jaws on your holiday here or abroad.
- Take part in a clean-up of your local beach. The Marine Conservation Society annual Beachwatch event takes place each year on the second weekend in September.
- Join the Great Eggcase Hunt and search for skate and ray eggcases (mermaid's purses) on the strandline. Report them to the Shark Trust. You can download a useful identification guide from their website www.eggcase.org.
- Keep your dogs from fouling the beach – clean up after them and remember some beaches are closed to dogs during certain times of the year. Check the notices on the beach or contact your local authority.
- Do not use sandy beaches or sand dunes for off-road motorcycling, as this causes great damage and erosion to these sensitive habitats. Report to the Police anyone you see doing this.
- When fishing along our coasts, take all your tackle home, including any which gets caught up on rocks or in seaweed.
- When bait-digging on sandy or muddy shores, fill the hole back in. If you collect soft crabs (peelers) for bait, follow the Seashore Code and carefully place back, the correct way up, each boulder you overturn.
- If you find any stranded or injured animals, please report them to the relevant authority on pages 212-213.

*Avoid buying marine curiosities on holiday here or abroad*

# Where to report your findings

All of the organisations below rely on volunteer wildlife recorders to report their sightings. This provides essential information and evidence on the distribution and abundance of marine wildlife around our coasts.

**By reporting your findings to the relevant organisation, you are contributing to:**

- Furthering understanding of our seashores
- Helping marine scientists in their research
- Aiding future management actions and plans.

### Jellyfish sightings

Marine Conservation Society Jellyfish survey. Submit your records of jellyfish strandings or offshore sightings online. A free jellyfish identification guide can be downloaded at www.mcsuk.org
The Ecojel project – assessing the opportunities and detrimental impacts of jellyfish in the Irish Sea. A free jellyfish identification card is available. Report your jellyfish sightings or strandings at www.jellyfish.ie/jellyfish_sight.asp

### Basking shark sightings

Marine Conservation Society Basking shark watch
www.mcsuk.org/baskingsharks

### Shark, skate and ray egg-case records

Shark Trust Great eggcase hunt. Search for shark, ray and skate egg-cases on the beach and submit your records online. There is also a free identification guide available.
www.sharktrust.org
www.eggcase.org

### Shark, skate and ray catches

Anglers can submit records of the shark, skate and ray species they catch to the catch database, to help increase understanding of local populations. There is a free identification guide online.
Email: sightings@sharktrust.org
If you catch a tagged skate or ray, please report this to your local Sea Fisheries Committee or the contact details on the tag, giving the date, area where the fish was caught and the tag number.

### Fish records

UK marine fish recording scheme
www.national-aquarium.co.uk/fishreports
National Marine Aquarium
Tel: 01752 600301
Fish recording: The fish recording website is designed to help fishermen, sea anglers, divers and sailors to record the fish species they have seen or caught.
www.fishrecording.info/

### Live strandings of whales, dolphins, porpoises or turtles

BDMLR hotline: 01825 765546
RSPCA hotline (England & Wales): 0300 1234 999
SSPCA hotline (Scotland): 03000 999 999 or your nearest location on Edinburgh 0131 339 0111, Aberdeen 01224 581236 or Inverness 01463 231191.
Welsh Marine Life Rescue (WMLR) on: 01646 692943.
If you find a live stranded whale or dolphin contact The Irish Whale & Dolphin Group immediately on: Tel: 021 904197 or 021 904053.

### Dead strandings of whales, dolphins, porpoises or turtles

The National Strandings Line: 0207 942 5155
Marine Environmental Monitoring in Wales www.strandings.com
University College Cork: 021 904197 or 021 904053
SAC Veterinary Services on: The National Strandings Line: 01463 243030
Marine Environmental Monitoring on The National Strandings Line: 01348 875000.

### General records of shore and marine life, non-native species and climate change indicator species

Marine Life Information Network for Britain and Ireland (*MarLIN*) Sealife survey Tel: 01752 255026 or send text and picture message to 07806 938789 with your name, contact details, what you saw, where you saw it and the date of your sighting. You can also email marlin@mba.ac.uk. Visit www.marlin.ac.uk/learningzone to submit sightings online.

### Non-native marine species

Report invasive marine species in Ireland by entering your records online under the 'Alien Watch' section at www.invasivespeciesireland.com
If you see a species that you think might be a new arrival then report where you saw it and email a photograph (or detailed description) to: alert_nonnative@ceh.ac.uk. You can also report any marine non-native species to the GB Non Native Species Secretariat https://secure.fera.defra.gov.uk/nonnativespecies/

### Stranded live seals

If you see a seal that may be abandoned, thin or ill, then call for advice and assistance:
BDMLR hotline: 01825 765546
RSPCA hotline: 0300 1234 999
If you find a live stranded seal in Ireland, contact the Irish Seal Sanctuary on: 01 8354370 or mobile 087 2333406.

### Report any unusual local shore or marine life sightings to:

- Your local biodiversity records centre
- Your local biodiversity partnership/forum
- Your local Wildlife Trust.
- Your local authority Biodiversity Officer
- The Porcupine Marine Natural History Society

# Further information

All of the following publications , websites and organisations were consulted during the writing of this book and are excellent sources of further information and aids to identifications.

## Books


**Brodie, J., Maggs, C.A. & John, D.M.** (eds). 2007. *Green Seaweeds of Britain and Ireland.* The British Phycological Society.

**Challinor, H., Murphy Wickers, S., Clark, J & Murphy, A.** 1999. *A beginners guide to Ireland's seashore.* Sherkin Island Marine Station.

**Crothers, J.** 1997. *A key to the major groups of British marine invertebrates.* Field Studies Vol 9, No 1. Field Studies Council.

**Crothers, J & M.** 1983. *A key to the crabs and crab-like animals of British inshore waters.* Reprinted 1988 with minor alterations from Field Studies 5 753-806. Field Studies Council.

**Hayward, P.J.** 1994. *Animals of sandy shores.* Naturalists handbooks 21. The Richmond Publishing Co Ltd.

**Hayward, P.J.** 1998. *Animals on seaweed.* Naturalists handbooks 9. The Richmond Publishing Co. Ltd.

**Hayward, P.J.** 2004. *Seashore.* The New Naturalist. Collins.

**Hayward, P., Nelson-Smith, T. & Shields, C.** 1996. Collins pocket guide. *Sea shore of Britain and northern Europe.* London: HarperCollins.

**Hayward, P.J & Ryland, J.S.** (eds). 2005. *Handbook of the marine fauna of NW Europe.* Oxford: Oxford University Press.

**Hiscock, S.** 1991. *A field guide to the British brown seaweeds.* Field Studies 5 (1979) 1-44. Field Studies Council.

**Kay, P. & Dipper, F.** 2009. *A Field Guide to the Marine Fishes of Wales and Adjacent Waters.* Marine Wildlife, Llanfairfechan.

**Kingsley, C.** 1890. *Glaucus or the Wonders of the Shore.* London: Macmillan

***MarLIN.*** 2003. *Sealife Surveys. Identification Guide for selected seashore Species.* Marine Biological Association of the UK, Plymouth.

**Naylor, P.** 2003. *Great British marine animals.* Sound Diving publications.

**Picton, B.** 1993. *A field guide to the shallow water echinoderms of the British Isles.* Immel Publishing Ltd.

**Picton, B.E. & Costello, M.J.** 1998. *BioMar* biotope viewer: a guide to marine habitats, fauna and flora of Britain and Ireland. [CD-ROM] Report.

**Picton, B. E. & Morrow, C.C.** 1994. *A field guide to the nudibranchs of the British Isles.* Immel Publishing Ltd.

**Preston-Mafham, R. & K.** 2004. *Seashore.* Collins Gem. Harper Collins publishers.

**Wheeler, W.** 1994. *Field Guide to the shore fishes of the British Isles.* Field studies 8 481-521. Field Studies Council.

**Wood, C.** 2005. *Seasearch guide to sea anemones and corals of Britain and Ireland.* Marine Conservation Society, Ross-on-Wye.

**Wood, C.** 2007. *Seasearch Observer's Guide to Marine Life of Britain and Ireland.* Marine Conservation Society, Ross-on-Wye.


## Organisations and useful websites

**Algaebase** – information on the algae of the world, including marine species. www.algaebase.org

**Amgueddfa Cymru – National Museum Wales** – the marine biodiversity section undertakes marine invertebrate research and outreach work. They have produced a free educational "Explore the Sea Floor" CD-ROM. www.museumwales.ac.uk

**Arkive** – a collection of videos, images and factfiles of the world's species. There is a section on marine invertebrates. www.arkive.org

**British Divers Marine Life Rescue** – dedicated to the rescue and well being of all marine animals in distress around the UK. www.bdmlr.org.uk

**British Marine Life Study Society** – reports of marine wildlife from all around the British Isles, with conservation initiatives as they affect the fauna and flora of the NE Atlantic Ocean. www.glaucus.org.uk

**Council for Nature Conservation and the Countryside** – advises the Department of Environment for Northern Ireland on matters affecting nature conservation and the countryside. www.cnccni.gov.uk

**Countryside Council for Wales (CCW)** – champions natural beauty, wildlife and the opportunity for outdoor enjoyment in Wales and its inshore waters. www.ccw.gov.uk

**Department of Communications, Environment and Natural Resources** – regulates, protects and develops the natural resources of Ireland. www.dcenr.gov.ie

**Encyclopedia of Marine life of Britain and Ireland** – this photographic guide covers a selection of the larger animals which live round the coasts of Britain and Ireland. It is intended for divers and marine biologists who need to be able to recognise species in situ. www.habitas.org.uk/marinelife

**Invasive species Ireland** – information on a range of non-native species, including marine. www.invasivespeciesireland.com

**Joint Nature Conservation Committee (JNCC)** – statutory advisor to the Government on UK and international nature conservation (including marine). www.jncc.gov.uk

**The Linnean Society of London** – the world's oldest active biological society. Their 'Synopses of the British fauna' include many marine titles. www.linnean.org

**Marine Aliens project** – a UK-wide co-ordinated research programme to look at the impacts of a selection of non-native marine invaders on indigenous species and ecosystems. www.marlin.ac.uk/marine_aliens

**Marine Biological Association (MBA)** – a learned society advancing marine science through research, communication and education. www.mba.ac.uk

**Marine Institute** – the national agency in Ireland responsible for marine research, technology development and innovation. www.marine.ie

**Marine Life Information Network of Britain and Ireland (*MarLIN*)** – provides information for marine environmental management, protection and education. It is a centre of excellence in spatially based and time-series marine biological information and supports good stewardship in the marine environment. www.marlin.ac.uk

**National Biodiversity Network (NBN) Gateway** – searchable datasets by species or location with distribution maps of marine life in Britain and Ireland. http://data.nbn.org.uk

**Natural England** – works to conserve, enhance and manage the natural environment of England. www.naturalengland.org.uk

**Natural History Museum** – information on species and a video on seaweed surveys in the Bristol Channel. www.nhm.ac.uk

**Northern Ireland Environment Agency** – protects, conserves and promotes the natural environment and built heritage of Northern Ireland. www.ni-environment.gov.uk

**Ocean Blue Marine Work Group Ireland** – information concerning the protection of Ireland's marine environment, sustainable use of its natural resources and conservation of its biodiveristy. www.oblue.utvinfonet.com

**Porcupine Marine Natural History Society** – an informal society interested in marine natural history and recording, particularly in the North East Atlantic region. www.pmnhs.co.uk

**Scottish Association for Marine Science (SAMS)** – promotes marine research and is committed to increasing knowledge and stewardship of the marine environment in Scotland. www.sams.ac.uk

**Scottish Natural Heritage** – promotes care for the natural heritage, wildlife, habitats, rocks and landscapes of Scotland. www.snh.org.uk

**Sea Slug Forum** – information on the nudibranchs, sea hares and sea slugs of the world. www.seaslugforum.net

**Sponges of Britain and Ireland** – identification guide to our sponges. www.habitas.org.uk/marinelife/sponge_guide

**United Kingdom Marine Climate Change Impacts Partnership (MCCIP)** – brings together scientists, government, its agencies and NGOs to provide co-ordinated advice on climate change impacts around our coast and in our seas. www.mccip.org.uk

**Wildlife Trusts** – voluntary organisation dedicated to conserving the full range of UK's habitats and species. There are 47 local Wildlife Trusts across the UK. www.wildlifetrusts.org

**World Register of Marine Species (WoRMS)** – aims to provide the most authoritative list of names of marine species globally. www.marinespecies.org

# Glossary

**Acrorhagi** aggressive organs of a sea anemone. They are inflated saclike structures bearing nematocysts that surround the collar below the tentacles. Acrorhagi can be elongated to come into contact with an intruder, whereupon they cause tissue death.

**Actinaria** sea anemones.

**Alcyonacea** soft corals.

**Annelida** segmented worms.

**Annual** once a year.

**Anthozoa** class of marine organisms in the phylum Cnidaria, embracing all forms of polyp including soft and stony corals and sea anemones. May be solitary or colonial, with or without an internal or external skeleton.

**Ascidian** sea squirt.

**Asteroidea** starfish.

**Ballast water** water carried in tanks on ships, which may breed alien or non-native species.

**Berried** term given to female crabs and lobsters when carrying eggs.

**Biodiversity** the variety of life forms.

**Biodiversity Action Plan** an internationally recognized programme addressing threatened species and habitats designed to protect and restore biological systems. The plans derive from the 1992 Convention on Biological Diversity (CBD). A Biodiversity Action Plan identifies the key biodiversity habitats and species.

**Blade** refers to the "leaves" of seaweed. Its main function is to provide a large surface for sunlight to be absorbed. It may also supports the reproductive structures of the plant.

**Byssus threads** threads produced by some bivalves, enabling them to attach themselves firmly to rocks and other structures.

**Carapace** the hard upper shell of a crustacean.

**Carnivore** a predator which feeds on animals.

**Cerata** extensions found on the back of some sea slugs. They are often brightly coloured and bear defensive organs.

**Chelipeds** the claw bearing appendages or pincers of decapod crustaceans.

**Chitin** substance which forms the exoskeleton or shell of crustaceans.

**Chlorophyceae** green seaweeds.

**Chlorophyll** green pigment present in most plants.

**Chordate** animal belonging to the phylum Chordata, which includes all those with a supporting rod of tissue (notochord or backbone) running down its body.

**Cirri** feeding appendages of barnacles.

**Cirripedia** barnacles.

**Classes** divisions in the classification of plants and animals.

**Cnidae** stinging cells unique to the phylum Cnidaria used in prey capture and defence.

**Cnidaria** a phylum of animals which includes jellyfish, corals, sea anemones and hydroids.

**Cold blooded** having a body temperature that rises or falls with the temperature of the surrounding environment.

**Colonial** organisms produced asexually which remain associated with each other; in many animals, retaining tissue contact with other polyps or zooids as a result of incomplete budding.

**Column** hollow, cylindrical body of anemone or coral polyp.

**Communities** groups of organisms occurring in a particular environment, interacting with each other and with the environment, and identifiable by means of ecological survey from other groups.

**Consumers** organisms that must eat other organisms for their energy.

**Corallum** relating to or resembling coral, especially any calcareous red alga impregnated with calcium carbonate.

**Crenulate** having a finely scalloped or notched outline or edge.

**Crinoidea** sea lilies.

**Crustacean** an animal with a hard skeleton on the outside, and many jointed legs.

**Decapod** a crustacean that has five pairs of walking legs. Decapod means 'ten legs'.

**Depositing shore** a sandy beach built up by deposition of sand particles.

**Dessication** removal of water; the process of drying.

**Detritus** fragmented particulate organic matter, derived from the decomposition of plant and animal remains.

**Ebb** outgoing or falling tide.

**Ecdysis** the brief period between moulting of the old exoskeleton and hardening of the new one, especially in Crustaceans.

**Echinoderm** a group of marine animals with spiny skins that includes starfish and sea urchins.

**Echinoidea** class of Phylum Echinodermata which includes sea urchins and heart urchins.

**Epifauna** Animals living on the surface of the seabed or the surface of seaweeds.

**Equinoctial spring tides** Highest tides of the year occurring shortly after the New and Full Moon closest to the equinoxes, taking place around 21st March and 23rd September.

**Eroding shores** rocky shores which are being worn away, by sea or wind.

**Eulittoral** the main part of the littoral zone characterized by limpets, barnacles, mussels, fucoid algae (other than those characteristic of the littoral fringe), with red algae often abundant on the lower part.

**Evert** to turn inside out, as in starfish which feed by pushing the stomach out through the mouth.

**Exoskeleton** hardened external skeleton or carapace in crabs for example.

**Exposed** a shore subject to strong wave action, and which is not sheltered.

**Filter feeding** a method of feeding used by some marine animals. Small particles of food are sieved or filtered out of the water.

**Flotsam** items washed on to the strandline by the sea, e.g. eggcases, driftwood, empty shells, fishing lines, plastic waste.

**Flow** movement of sea water when the tide comes in.

**Food chain** a sequence showing the feeding relationships between organisms in a habitat.

**Food web** a diagram showing the relationships between organisms in several food chains.

**Frond** the leaf like part of a seaweed.

**Fucoxanthin** most brown algae contain the pigment fucoxanthin, which is responsible for the distinctive greenish brown color that gives them their name.

**Gastropod** a type of mollusc, usually with a single shell and a muscular foot used for movement eg sea snails.

**Habitat** the place in which a plant or animal lives.

**Haptera** root like structures of macroalgae holdfasts.

**Herbivore** organism which feeds on plants, including phytoplankton.

**Hermaphrodite** having both male and female reproductive organs in the same individual.

**Holdfast** an attachment structure that anchors large algae e.g. kelps to the substratum. It resembles a collection of roots, but has no nutrient gathering role.

**Hydroid** a general term for members of the Class Hydrozoa, and includes 'sea firs'.

**Hydrozoa** the Class Hydrozoa (of Phylum Cnidaria) are characterized by large colonies of simple polyps which vary in structure. The general form is of a central mouth and buccal cavity surrounded by stinging tentacles.

**Infauna** benthic animals which live within the seabed.

**Interstitial spaces** relating to the system of cavities and channels formed by the spaces between grains in sediment such as sand.

**Intertidal zone** the area between the high and low tide mark that is covered and uncovered by the tide twice a day.

**Invasive species** species that achieve the fastest and greatest dispersal, aided by both natural and 'man made' transport, e.g. attached to boats docking in marinas. Such non-native species have potentially the greatest impact on native communities.

**Invertebrates** creatures that do not have a backbone.

**Iridescence** an oily or brilliant shine seen on some seaweeds and animals when underwater.

**Lamina** in seaweeds, a flattened structure that is somewhat leaf like.

**Lichen** a fungus, that grows symbiotically with algae. This results in a composite organism that characteristically forms a crustlike or branching growth on rocks in the splash zone.

**Littoral** the area affected by the rise and fall of the tides.

**Lower shore** the lowest part of the shore at the seaward end, uncovered by the tide.

**Macrofauna** living organisms which inhabit beaches and which are retained by a 0.5mm sieve.

**Malacostraca** largest order of crustaceans including crabs, lobsters, prawns and shrimps.

**Mantle** soft outer body wall of a mollusc.

**Marine algae** green, brown and red seaweeds.

**Meiofauna** tiny marine creatures living between sand grains.

**Micro-habitat** a small area with physical and ecological characteristics that distinguish it from its immediate surrounding area e.g. crevices, rockpools, boulders.

**Middle shore** the area of the shore between the highest and lowest levels.

**Moderately exposed shore** shores which are neither sheltered nor pounded by extreme wave action (exposed).

**Mollusc** member of the phylum Mollusca. Invertebrate animals with soft unsegmented bodies, a muscular foot, and a body enclosed in a mantle. Most molluscs have a calcareous outer shell.

**Neap tides** the lowest high tide of the lunar month, occurring near the first and third quarters of the moon phases between spring tides.

**Nematocysts** structures involved in the stinging mechanism for defence and prey capture, unique to Cnidarians.

**Notochord** skeletal tube running from front to back in some simple chordates e.g. in the larvae of sea squirts.

**Nudibranch** sea slugs, most lack a shell, mantle cavity and gills, and breathe through the body surface. They are noted for their often extraordinary colours and striking forms.

**Omnivore** an animal that eats both plants and animals.

**Operculum** a horny disc that covers the shell opening in some gastropods when the foot is pulled in, to prevent the animal inside from drying out.

**Ophiuroidea** a class of the Phylum Echinodermata which includes the Brittlestars.

**Opistobranch mollusc** highly colourful marine gastropods of the suborder Nudibranchia (sea slugs). Opistobranch means "gills to the right and behind the heart".

**Order** major subdivision of a class.

**Osculum (plural Oscula)** in sponges, a large opening to the outside for letting water out of the internal water chamber.

**OSPAR Priority Species** The Convention for the Protection of the Marine Environment of the North East Atlantic (OSPAR).

**Osteichthyes** also called bony fish, are a taxonomic class of fish. The vast majority of fish are osteichthyes.

**Ostia** a series of tiny pores all over the body of a sponge that let water into the sponge. One of these is called an ostium.

**Paddleworm** any of a family of green blue faintly iridescent active marine polychaete worms of the genus Phyllodoce, having paddle shaped swimming lobes, found under stones on the shore.

**Parapodia** a sort of "false foot" formed by extension of the body cavity. Polychaetes have parapodia in addition to their legs, and these provide extra help in locomotion. They are also found in opisthobranch (nudibranch) molluscs.

**Pedicellariae** minute moveable stalked pincers projecting from the skin of some Echinoderms, particularly of the class Asteroidea. They are found near the base of spines and used mainly to keep the body surface clear of encrusting organisms.

**Peduncle** in Crustaceans, a stalk like part of the body. In some Molluscs e.g. goose barnacles, it is a fleshy stalk used to attach the animal to the substrate.

**Pelecypoda** this class contains the molluscs known as bivalves, including mussels, oysters, scallops, and clams. All have shells composed of two valves.

**Perennial** a plant or marine alga that is active throughout the year and can live for many years.

**Phaeophyceae** the Phaeophyceae or brown algae, is a large group of mostly marine multicellular algae, including many seaweeds of colder Northern Hemisphere waters. They play an important role in marine environments both as food, and for the habitats they form.

**Phycocyanin** a pigment which absorbs orange and red light.

**Phycoerythrin** a red protein present in red algae. Phycoerythrin absorbs red and purple wavelengths and reflects green.

**Phyla** the first division used when classifying organisms (single = phylum) composed of a number of classes.

**Phytoplankton** microscopic plant life, usually algae, which drift in the sea and form basis of food chains and webs. They are the food of zooplankton (microscopic marine animals).

**Plates** shells that cover the body of a barnacle or a chiton.

**Pleopods** swimming legs of crustaceans.

**Polychaete** marine segmented worm characterized by extensions called parapodia that bear bundles of bristles.

**Polyp** an individual in a colony of animals e.g. corals. A polyp usually consists of a sac like body with tentacles surrounding the mouth.

**Porifera** sponges (poriferans) are very simple animals that live permanently attached to a location in the water.

**Proboscis** a slender, tubular feeding and sucking organ of some worms and molluscs.

**Producers** plants are called producers because only they can manufacture food from inorganic raw materials.

**Prosobranch mollusc** the largest subclass of the Gastropoda. The group includes marine snails. Prosobranch means "gills in front of the heart".

**Radially symmetrical** in echinoderms, symmetry of organism where body parts are equally arranged around a median vertical axis which passes through the mouth. There is no front and rear end and therefore no left and right sides.

**Radula** part of the feeding apparatus in gastropod molluscs.

**Radular ribbon** a continuously secreted ribbon bearing rows of hardened teeth, used for grazing in gastropod molluscs.

**Rhinophores** in nudibranchs, paired sensory tentacles on head, primarily used for smell and taste. The shape varies greatly from one species to another.

**Rhodophyceae** a large class of plants, commonly called red algae.

**Sacoglossan** are a taxonomic order of opisthobranch gastropod molluscs including the sea hare.

**Scavengers** animal feeding on carrion.

**Scleractinia** hard or stony corals.

**Sea firs** Hydroids, or sea firs, are the simplest of the stinging celled animals.

**Seaweed** seaweed is often (mistakenly) referred to as a plant, but these red, green and brown algae do not have roots, stems or leaves like plants. They anchor themselves to rocks using structures called 'holdfasts'.

**Sediment feeder** also known as a deposit feeder. An organism that derives its nutrition by consuming some fraction of soft sediment.

**Sessile** permanently attached or fixed; not free moving.

**Sheltered shore** a shore less exposed to strong wave action than an exposed shore.

**Solitary** living alone.

**Species** a group of individual animals which is the basic unit of the classification system.

**Species Action Plan** part of a local Biodiversity Action Plan.

**Spicules** minute, pointed structures forming part of the skeleton especially used for identification of sponges.

**Splash zone** the area at the top of the shore that is not covered by the tide at any time but is made wet by salt spray from wave action.

**Sporophyll** in seaweeds, additional structures produced by some kelps above the holdfast and below the blade.

**Spring tides** a tide with the largest difference in water level between high and low tide, occurring every two weeks.

**Stipe** in seaweeds, the stalk or stem which connects the holdfast to the frond.

**Strandline** the area along the high tide mark on the beach where seaweed and other debris collects.

**Sub-littoral** the zone exposed to air only at its upper limit by the lowest spring tides i.e. the area below low tide level.

**Supralittoral fringe** the part of the seashore lying above extreme high water mark of spring tides.

**Suspension feeder** animal such as a barnacle or sponge that feeds by filtering particles of organic matter from sea water.

**Taxonomic order** the classification of organisms into related groups.

**Telson** the 'tail' of a crustacean.

**Test** the 'shell' of a sea urchin.

**Tubercle** a small rounded swelling found on the dorsal surface of some species of nudibranchs.

**Tunicate** also known as urochordates is the group of sac-like filter feeding sea squirts.

**Umbilicus** opening or hole at base of some gastropod shells.

**Upper eulittoral** the upper shore.

**Upper shore** the highest part of the shore covered by the incoming tide.

**Urochordate** a chordate of the subphylum Urochordata comprising the tunicates or sea squirts.

**Valve** the individual shell of a bivalve.

**Verrucae** series of suckers on column of some sea anemones.

**Vertebrate** animal with backbone or spinal column.

**Whorl** a single turn of a spiral shell.

**Zonation** the positioning of animals and plants on the shore, relative to the level of the tide.

**Zooid** individual animal of colonial species especially in sea squirts.

**Zooxanthellae** tiny photosynthesizing algae found in the tissues of some corals and anemones.

# Acknowledgements

Jacques-Yves Cousteau was my very first inspiration for all things marine, through his wonderful television programmes and books. However, if it wasn't for my parents' love of the natural world, I would not have been introduced to the joys of the seashore and rockpooling at a very early age. I thank them for encouraging me to pursue a career in natural history. My mother, father and brother accompanied me on various 'Seashore Safaris' and assisted with everything from finding species to carrying equipment and spent many hours proofreading drafts of the book. They have given me enormous encouragement throughout my life and I dedicate this book to them.

My husband Michael has been a great support during the writing of this book. He has endured many hours of my rockpooling expeditions and 'seashore talk'. His tremendous encouragement and patience, and his help working as my camera assistant and extra pair of hands and eyes on the shore, deserves my sincere thanks.

I am indebted to my many friends at the Marine Life Information Network for Britain and Ireland and the Marine Biological Association, together with many other marine and coastal friends and acquaintances, too numerous to mention, for help and advice.

To Dr Keith Hiscock and Iolo Williams – many thanks for agreeing to write the forewords, and for your very kind words.

Dr Richard Kirby (MBA), generously allowed the use of his plankton image on page 25.

Sincere thanks also to all my friends, family and work colleagues, too numerous to mention but you know who you are, for their suggestions and comments on the proofs, and for providing book testimonials.

To Dr Andrew Mackie (Amgueddfa Cymru – National Museum Wales), a huge thank you for your detailed proof-checking and many constructive suggestions.

Thanks to my publishers at Graffeg, and in particular to Peter Gill, Vanessa Bufton, Diana Edwards and Joana Rodrigues for believing in my idea for the book and for allowing me to progress with it. I am so pleased that our many hours of design meetings have finally come together as this eye-catching guide.

The wonderful reviews of the first edition have made all my efforts worthwhile!

Thanks to the Welsh Books Council for awarding an Authors grant towards the production of the book.

Cameras Underwater (especially Dave Glanfield), were very generous in sponsoring me with a Canon Ixus compact camera and underwater housing.

Finally, to all the amazing animals of the shore who have allowed me to be a part of their extraordinary world, and have held my fascination for over 35 years, thank you for giving me a lifetime of pleasure.

I am hopeful that with better understanding of marine conservation issues and measures, future generations will continue to be able to enjoy investigating our marine and seashore life.

# Index


## A

*Abra alba* 66, 145
*Acanthochitona crinita* 122
*Acteon tornatilis* 66, 73, 140
*Actinia equina* 34, 49, 91
*Actinia fragacea* 89
*Aeolidia papillosa* 51, 138
*Aeolidiella alderi* 138
*Alaria esculenta* 39, 195
*Alcyonidium diaphanum* 71
Alder's necklace shell 73, 135
Algae,
  Brown 190–194
  Encrusting coralline 197
  Green 188
  Red 196
*Alitta virens* 102
American oyster drill 206
*Ammodytes tobianus* 178
*Amphipholis squamata* 57, 160
Anemone,
  Beadlet 7, 28, 34, 49, 89, 91
  Dahlia 46, 47, 83
  Daisy 93
  Elegant 46, 47, 91
  Gem 45, 89
  Jewel 49
  Snakelocks 36, 51, 90, 112, 203
  Strawberry 89, 203
*Anemonia viridis* 36, 90
Animal life 76
*Anomia ephippium* 143
*Ansates pellucida* 53, 126
*Antedon bifida* 155
*Aplysia punctata* 137
*Archidoris pseudoargus* 45, 55, 139
*Arenicola marina* 103
*Ascophyllum nodosum* 192
*Asterias rubens* 47, 157
*Asterina gibbosa* 158
*Asterina phylactica* 159
*Astropecten irregularis* 60, 165
*Aulactinia verrucosa* 45, 89
Australian tube worm 206, 209
*Austrominius modestus* 107, 206

## B

*Balanophyllia regia* 86
*Balanus crenatus* 107
*Balanus perforatus* 49, 107
Ballan wrasse 177
Banded carpet shell 72
Banded venus 72, 145
Banded wedge shell 60, 67, 134, 149
Barnacle,
  Acorn 28, 32, 33, 107
  Buoy 59
  Common Goose 70, 71
  Volcano 37, 74, 107, 203
Barnacles 106
Beachcombing 68
Beach litter 200, 204, 205
*Bifurcaria bifurcata* 191, 203
Bivalves 142
*Botrylloides leachi* 168
*Botrylloides violaceus* 206, 207
*Botryllus schlosseri* 55, 57, 170
Boulders 54, 56
Brittle star,
  Little 57, 160
Brittlestar,
  Common 37, 57, 161
Brittlestars 160
Brown shrimp 63
Bryozoans or sea mats 150
*Buccinum undatum* 135
Butterfish 176
By-the-wind-sailor 59

## C

*Calliostoma zizyphinum* 55, 129
*Cancer pagurus* 36, 47, 113
*Carcinus maenas* 114
*Caryophyllia smithii* 87
*Catenella caespitosa* 31, 199
*Cerastoderma edule* 144
*Cereus pedunculatus* 93
*Chamelea striatula* 145
Chitons 122
*Chlamys varia* 142
*Chlorophyceae* 188, 216
*Chondrus crispus* 34, 196
*Chrysaora hysoscella* 59
*Chthamalus montagui* 107
*Chthamalus stellatus* 107
*Ciliata mustela* 53, 175
*Ciocalypta penicillus* 81
*Cladophora rupestris* 189
*Clausinella fasciata* 145
*Clavelina lepadiformis* 169
Climate change 202, 203
Cnidaria 82, 216
Cockle,
  Common 41, 144
  Spiny 41, 73
*Codium tomentosum* 189
*Colpomenia peregrina* 185, 206
Common or estuary ragworm 95
Common otter shell 146
Connemara clingfish 51
Conservation 200
Coral,
  Devonshire cup 49, 87
  Scarlet and gold star 49, 86
*Corallina officinalis* 34, 51, 197
Corals 86
Coral weed 34, 37, 51, 197
*Corella eumyota* 206, 207
Corkwing wrasse 37, 174
*Corynactis viridis* 49
*Corystes cassivelaunus* 61, 118
Cowrie,
  Arctic or northern 125
  Spotted or European 125
Crab,
  Angular 6, 105
  Broad-clawed porcelain 35, 57, 114
  Chinese mitten 206
  Common hermit 51, 63, 113
  Common or Spiny spider 74, 112
  Common shore 35, 41, 114
  Edible or Brown 36, 113
  Furrowed or Montagu's 111, 203
  Hairy 109
  Leach's spider 112
  Long-clawed porcelain 57
  Long-legged spider 53, 110
  Masked 41, 61, 67, 118
  Pennant's swimming 41, 66, 119
  Risso's 111
  South-claw or small hermit 60, 119
  Spiny spider 112
  Velvet swimming 37, 111
Crabs 108
*Crangon crangon* 63, 117
*Crassostrea gigas* 206, 209
*Crenilabrus melops* 174
*Crepidula fornicata* 206, 208
Crevices 44
Crinoids 154
Crustaceans 104
Cushion star or Starlet 158
Cuvie 39, 195
*Cystoseira tamariscifolia* 190

## D

Dabberlocks 37, 39, 195
Dead man's fingers 49, 87
*Dendrodoa grossularia* 47, 55, 169
*Dictyota dichotoma* 190
*Diodora graeca* 126
*Diogenes pugilator* 60, 119
Dog whelk 45, 49, 132, 183,
  Netted or reticulated 135
*Donax vittatus* 149
*Dosima fascicularis* 59
*Dosinia exoleta* 148
Dulse 36, 199
*Dynamena pumila* 85
*Dysidia fragilis* 55, 79

## E

*Echinocardium cordatum* 61, 165
Echinoderms 152
*Echinus esculentus* 163
Egg-cases,
  Shark and ray 59
Eggs 180
Egg wrack wool 198
*Electra pilosa* 150
*Elysia viridis* 53, 136

*Ensis siliqua* 61, 147
*Entelerus aequoreus* 174
Epifauna 40, 60, 217
Equipment 13
*Eulalia viridis* 97
*Eurynebria complanata* 62
Exposure 21

## F

*Facelina auriculata* 36, 138
False Irish moss 35, 198
Faroe sunset shell 149
*Ficopomatus enigmaticus* 206, 209
Fifteen-spined stickleback 172
Fish 172
Five-bearded rockling 53, 175
Flatworm,
  Candy striped 97
*Flustrellidra hispida* 151
Food chains 24, 25, 217
Food webs 24, 25, 217
Football jersey worm 96
*Fucus serratus* 36, 55, 186, 192
*Fucus spiralis* 33, 186, 192
*Fucus vesiculosus* 34, 85, 186, 193
Furbelows 39, 195

## G

*Galathea squamifera* 57, 114
*Galathea strigosa* 45
*Gari fervensis* 149
Gastropods 124, 217
Geology 21
*Gibbula cineraria* 51, 128
*Gibbula umbilicalis* 34, 129
*Goneplax rhomboides* 105
*Grantia compressa* 47, 81
Grey seal 59
Gutweed 33, 189

## H

Habitats 42
*Halichoerus grypus* 59
*Halichondria panicea* 36, 47, 49, 80
*Haliclystus auricula* 53
*Halidrys siliquosa* 191
Harpoon weed 206
Health and Safety 14
*Hediste diversicolor* 95
*Hemimycale columella* 80
*Himanthalia elongata* 193
*Hinia reticulata* 135
*Hippolyte varians* 117
*Homarus gammarus* 115
Hydroids or sea firs 53, 84
*Hymeniacidon perleve* 79

## I

*Inachus phalangium* 112
Infauna 40, 60, 217
Intertidal zone 154, 217
Irish moss or Carragheen 34, 51, 196

## J

Jellyfish,
  Compass 59
  Dustbin lid or barrel 71

## K

Keelworm 94, 98
Kelp 38, 186, 187
King Rag worm 102

## L

*Labrus bergylta* 177
*Lagis koreni* 102
*Laminaria digitata* 39, 194
*Laminaria hyperborea* 39, 195
*Lanice conchilega* 61, 101
*Lepadogaster candolii* 51
*Lepadogaster lepadogaster* 36, 173
*Lepas anatifera* 71
*Lepidochitona cinerea* 123
*Lepidonotus clava* 97
*Leptosynapta inhaerens* 153
Lesser sand eel 178
Lichen,
  Black tar 31
  Crab's eye 31
  Yellow 31
Lichens 30, 31, 217
*Lichina pygmaea* 31
*Ligia oceanica* 59
Limpet,
  American slipper 206, 208
  Blue-rayed 37, 53, 126
  Common 28, 34, 127
  Common keyhole 126
*Lineus longissimus* 96
*Lipophrys pholis* 45, 177
*Lithophyllum* 197
*Lithothamnion* 197
Little cuttlefish 63
*Littorina littorea* 130
*Littorina obtusata* 34, 130
*Littorina saxatilis* 33, 45, 131
Lobster,
  Common 115
  Squat 45, 57, 114
Lobsters 108
*Lomentaria articulata* 197
Lugworm 41, 103
*Luidia ciliaris* 157
*Lutraria lutraria* 146

## M

*Macropodia rostrata* 53, 110
*Mactra stultorum* 61, 148
*Maja squinado* 112
*Marthasterias glacialis* 45, 159
*Mastocarpus stellatus* 198
*Melarhaphe neritoides* 33, 131
Molluscs 120
*Morchellium argus* 169
Mussel,
  Common or Blue 35, 143
*Mytilus edulis* 143

## N

Necklace shell 41, 67, 134
*Necora puber* 111
*Nerophis lumbriciformis* 57, 177
Non-native species 206
*Nucella lapillus* 45, 49, 132

## O

Oarweed or Tangle 194
*Obelia longissima* 85
*Ocenebra erinacea* 131
*Ochrelechia parella* 31
*Onchidoris bilamellata* 107
*Ophiothrix fragilis* 57, 161
*Ophiura albida* 66, 164
*Ophiura ophiura* 165
Orange peel bryozoan 151
Orange sheath tunicate 206, 207
*Osilinus lineatus* 34, 128
*Osmundea pinnatifida* 196
*Ostrea edulis* 143
Overhangs 48
Oyster,
  Native, Common or Flat 143
  Portuguese or Pacific 206, 209
  Saddle 143
Oystercatcher 60
Oyster drill or European sting winkle 131
Oyster thief 185, 206

## P

*Pagurus bernhardus* 51, 63, 113
*Palaemon serratus* 116
*Palmaria palmata* 36, 199
*Pawsonia saxicola* 153
*Patella vulgata* 34, 127
*Pelvetia canaliculata* 33, 186, 193
Pepper dulse 35, 196
Periwinkle,
  Common or Edible 35, 72, 130
  Flat 34, 72, 130
  Rough 28, 33, 45, 131
  Small 28, 33, 131
Phaeophyceae 190, 218
*Pholis gunnellus* 176
*Pilumnus hirtellus* 109
Pipefish,
  Snake 37, 174
  Worm 29, 57, 177, 183, 203
*Pisidia longicornis* 57
Plaice 63
*Pleurobrachia pileus* 70
*Pleuronectes platessa* 63
Pod razor shell 61, 72, 147
*Polinices catenus* 134
*Polinices pulchellus* 135
*Polysiphonia lanosa* 198
*Pomatoceros lamarcki* 98
*Pomatoschistus minutus* 63, 179
*Porcellana platycheles* 57, 114
Porifera 78
*Porphyra umbilicalis* 199

*Portumnus latipes* 119
Prawn,
Chameleon 117
Common 25, 51, 116
Prawns 116
*Prostheceraeus vittatus* 97
*Psammechinus miliaris* 36, 57, 162
Puffin 178
Pullet carpet shell 73, 148
Purple heart urchin 61
Purple laver 199

## Q

Quiz 64, 204

## R

*Ramalina siliquosa* 31
Rayed artemis 148
Rayed trough shell 61, 67, 72, 148
Razor shell 41, 67, 72
Report findings 212
*Rhizostoma octopus* 71
Rhodophyceae 196, 219
Rockpools 50
Rosy feather-star 154, 155

## S

*Sabellaria alveolata* 55, 99
*Saccharina latissima* 39, 194
*Saccorhiza polyschides* 39, 195
*Sagartia elegans* 47, 91
*Sagartiogeton undatus* 93
Sand goby 63, 179
Sandhopper 40, 59
Sand mason worm 41, 61, 101
Sand star 60, 75, 165
*Sargassum muticum* 206, 208
Scale worm 97
Sea anemones 88
Sea chervil 71
Sea cucumber 153
Sea gherkin 153
Sea gooseberry 70
Sea hare 137, 182, 183
Sea ivory 31
Sea lemon 55, 139, 182, 183
Sea lettuce 51, 188
Sea mat,
Hairy 150
Sea oak 51, 191
Sea potato 61, 162, 165
Sea scorpion,
Long-spined 175
Seashore Code 15
Sea slater 40, 59
Sea slug,
Grey 51, 138, 182, 183
Sea slugs 136
Sea snails 124
Sea squirt,
Baked bean or Gooseberry 169
Leathery 206, 207
Light bulb 37, 169
Star ascidian 55, 57, 170
Sea squirts or Ascidians 168
Sea urchin,
Common or Edible 163
Green or Shore 36, 57, 162
Sea urchins 162
Seaweeds 184
*Semibalanus balanoides* 107
*Sepiola atlantica* 63
Shanny or Common blenny 45, 177, 183
Shell guide 72
Shore,
Lower 36
Middle 34
Rocky 22
Sandy 22
Upper 32
Shore clingfish 7, 36, 173, 203
Shore urchin test 74
Shrimp,
Brown 63, 117
Shrimps 116
Small-spotted catshark 182, 183
Sole,
Common or Dover 63, 179
*Solea solea* 63, 179
*Spatangus purpureus* 61
*Spinachia spinachia* 172
*Spirobis spirobis* 98
Sponge,
Breadcrumb 35, 36, 47, 49, 80
Crater 80
Golf ball 81
Pencil 81
Purse 37, 47, 81
Sponges 78
Stalked jellyfish 53
Star ascidian 55, 57, 168, 170
Starfish 156,
Common 37, 47, 157
Seven-armed 157
Spiny 7, 45, 159
Strandline 58, 62
Strandline beetle 62
Striped venus clam 67, 73, 145
*Styela clava* 206, 207
Sub-littoral fringe 36, 163, 186
Sugar kelp or Sea belt 39, 194
Surge gullies 46

## T

*Talitrus saltator* 59
Tangle or Oarweed 194
*Taurulus bubalis* 175
Tellin,
Thin 146
*Tellina tenuis* 146
*Tethya aurantium* 81
Thongweed 29, 37, 193
Threats 202
Tidal ranges 20
Tides 20
*Tonicella rubra* 122
Top shell,
Flat or purple 34, 129
Grey 51, 72, 128
Painted 29, 37, 55, 72, 129
Toothed or Thick 128
*Tricellaria inopinata* 206, 209
*Trivia arctica* 125
*Trivia monacha* 55, 125
Tube worms 94, 98, 99, 101, 209
*Tubulanus annulatus* 96
Tunicates 166
*Turbicellepora magnicostata* 151

## U

*Ulva intestinalis* 33, 189
*Ulva lactuca* 51, 188
Urchin,
Heart 41, 165
*Urticina felina* 47, 83

## V

Variegated scallop 73, 142
*Velella velella* 59
Velvet horn 189
*Venerupsis senegalensis* 148
*Ventromma halecioides* 85
*Verrucaria maura* 31
Vertebrates 166

## W

Wakame 206
Whelk
Common 72, 75, 135, 182, 183
Wireweed 206, 208
Worm,
Bootlace 96
Green leaf 97, 183
Honeycomb 37, 55, 99
Sand mason 41, 61, 101
Trumpet 102
Worms 94
Wrack,
Bladder 34, 186, 187, 193
Channelled 28, 32, 33, 186, 187, 193
Egg 187
Egg or Knotted 192
Serrated 187
Serrated, Saw or Toothed 36, 192
Spiral 28, 32, 33, 186, 187, 192
Tamarisk weed or rainbow 190

## X

*Xantho incisus* 111
*Xantho pilipes* 111
*Xanthoria parietina* 31

## Z

Zonation 26,
Rocky shore 28
Sandy shore 40
Seaweed 186
Zone,
Laminarian 38
Splash 30

Published by Graffeg
First published 2010
Revised edition 2011

ISBN 9781905582525

Seashore Safaris written and photographed by Judith Oakley.

Graffeg,
Radnor Court,
256 Cowbridge Road East,
Cardiff, CF5 1GZ Wales UK.
T: +44 (0)29 2078 5156
sales@graffeg.com
www.graffeg.com

Graffeg are hereby identified as the authors of this work in accordance with section 77 of the Copyrights, Designs and Patents Act 1988.

Distributed by the Welsh Books Council www.cllc.org.uk
castellbrychan@cllc.org.uk

A CIP Catalogue record for this book is available from the British Library.

Designed and produced by
Peter Gill & Associates
sales@petergill.com
www.petergill.com



**Graffeg books**

Graffeg books are available from all good books shops and online from www.graffeg.com

Our list includes the following titles:

- Coastline Wales
- Landscape Wales
- About Wales
- About south Wales
- About mid Wales
- About north Wales
- About west Wales
- Welsh National Opera
- Food Wales – a second helping
- Food Wales eating out guide
- Bryan Webb's Kitchen: Tyddyn Llan
- Celtic Cuisine
- Golf Wales
- Skomer Island
- Caldey Island
- Pembrokeshire David Wilson
- Discovering Welsh Gardens
- Discovering Welsh Houses
- Pocket Wales Landscape Wales
- Pocket Wales Coast Wales
- Pocket Wales Castles of Wales
- Pocket Wales Mountain Wales
- Village Wales
- Market Towns Wales
- Senedd